WANTED - FEROCIOUS MEN OF PRAYER

DAVID LEE MARTIN

CONTENTS

ENDORSEMENTS

"Truly inspiring! I believe this book is a signpost to the next step of the end time harvest of the nations. After reading, I was refreshed and taken deeper in my relationship with God through prayer. I have been privileged to witness the many talents and great accomplishments in David's life, and I am sure it all comes out of his dedication to the life of prayer." – *Klemen Vidic, Senior Pastor, International Network of Churches, Slovenia*

"'Wanted- Ferocious Men of Prayer', is a very powerful book that is needed in this day and age. David Lee Martin's way of spurring men to devote and dedicate their lives to prayer is without a doubt, a success. This book will open spiritual doors that will heighten your faith and personal relationship with God." – *David Nappa, Pastor, Bread of Life Church, Malta.*

"There is a real strength in this book. It will encourage you to grasp prayer with both hands and hold on tight because it is going to be the ride of a lifetime. God's purpose is to transform us into the image of his Son. *'Wanted - Ferocious Men of Prayer'* offers guidance that will lead to transformation and change so God can powerfully influence our environment and the nations we pray for." – *Andrew Timms, Senior Pastor, Destiny Life Church in Bournemouth, England*

"Like E M bounds books on prayer, David's book is sure to become a classic on prayer for future generations. This book has been conceived through decades of the author's abiding in the secret place. *"Wanted - Ferocious men of Prayer"* will surely challenge and set you ablaze to embrace your uttermost privilege and responsibility, that is to be a man of prayer." – *Mario Otero, Director, Gospel Action International, Spain*

FOREWORD
BY ROD ANDERSON

The Father always rewards diligent seekers with greater depth of acquaintance with Him, greater revelation from Him, and the discipline simply brings you to a place where a beautiful peace, serenity and glory that begins to occupy your soul.

This is the rest that Jesus promised would be ours as we take His yoke upon us.

Everything needs prayer; our cities, our counties, our nation, our schools, our families, our political scene, our media world and definitely our church world.

Everyone will agree that we need more prayer, but when will we act upon this conviction?

This book is a call to God's men, to discover their true priority, which is building God's Kingdom through a shameless prayer lifestyle!

In the heart of a man is a God-planted "holy aggression". The sad truth that many, if not the majority of men, have been emasculated through the fear of man. They don't truly know the "fear of the Lord." They haven't discovered the power that comes with personal consecration to God.

Too many men are simply lackadaisical in their attitudes towards life. There is an unmistakable call for an awakening of the warrior spirit that God has put in every man's heart. Men who will confront evil in any form, remembering that what you don't confront, you'll ultimately contain.

Be encouraged. Be motivated. Step into the glory of a disciplined prayer life that will lead you into Father's delights.

This book will do this for you, and more.

READ this book, not casually, but with intention. Be assured, a reward WILL come to your life, as this is Father's promise to us all.

Rod Anderson

The Prayer Foundation co-founder
Senior Pastor, Commonwealth Church London

I WOULD SELL THE FARM TO BUY THIS FIELD!

INTRODUCTION

> "If Bible Christianity is to survive the
> present world upheaval, we shall need
> to have a fresh revelation of the
> greatness and the beauty of Jesus.... He
> alone can raise our cold hearts to
> rapture and restore again the art of true
> worship." — A.W. Tozer

A story is told in Scripture of a pasture so precious that the man who discovered its treasures was willing to sell all else to possess its secrets.

Worth a thousand farms, and all else besides, nothing can compare to the presence of God becoming real in your everyday experience.

The pursuits and ambitions of modern life pale in

comparison. This one pursuit remains timeless and unmatched in the rewards it offers.

Prayer!

Once tasted, the joy of prayer is a discovery that becomes a sell-all proposition.

The man in our story was willing to offer everything else he held precious to gain something of infinitely greater value.

> "The Kingdom of Heaven is like a treasure that a man discovered hidden in a field. In his excitement, he hid it again and sold everything he owned to get enough money to buy the field." (Matthew 13:44 NLT)

As a modern man, life will pull your heart in many directions seeking to hook you on promises of happiness and fulfilment. In the fast-paced digital world a gaggle of voices endlessly drags our splintered attention from one thing to another seeking satisfaction.

But fulfilment doesn't reside in things. It's not packaged like the holiday you think will make your soul sing.

You don't need to travel to taste the fullness of joy or the magnificent ring of victory. It's right here.

Like the field in Jesus' parable, the true riches are hidden right under your feet. In the gritty soil of your manly heart there is a treasure aching to be found.

COUNTING THE COST

The cost to taste the wonders that a rich and satisfying prayer life offers is time.

Time is life spilling through your fingers. Where will you choose to spend it?

The field is ready for the taking. Present and waiting for your presence.

Man of God, Jesus is real, God is speaking, and the Holy Spirit is with you, in you, and leading you deeper!

No greater service can be rendered to mankind, no greater skill encouraged or obtained. The mystery of prayer remains only mysterious to those who have never taken the time to dig into its treasures.

Once you start digging, taking time behind the curtain, shutting out the noise and tumult, you'll begin to see the beautiful simplicity found only in the face of the Saviour.

To look upon Jesus, to taste his goodness, to partake of His victory and peace, is a field I'll gladly sell my farm for!

Reputation is a small price to pay to enter His courts.

Opportunities and pursuits on the periphery of the field of prayer seem pallid in comparison to the fruitful delights He offers His lovers.

Anaemic avenues leading to glamor, fame, or fortune, are dirt roads to nowhere compared to the highway of holiness pulling hungry seekers into the joy of His presence.

Yes, this field is worth all you own. This field of uncultivated power, joy, peace, and love, is incomparable. Let your hand take the plough and drive firm furrows into the soil of relationship with the King. Let your lips sow seeds of adoration that grow up into fruit-bearing trees of healing. Let your tears water the ground in repentance and thanksgiving.

Let this favoured field burst forth in the warm light of God's grace through Jesus Christ.

It will be your sanctuary from the storm.

Its treasures will satisfy your craving for significance.

Its furrows, vines, and fruits, will satiate your hunger for a courageous life that counts.

No other field I have ever found has so fascinated my heart, so fully captured my curiosity, so completely possessed anything closely worthy of lifelong pursuit, as the beautiful, indescribable, delightful, majestic field of prayer.

Have you visited your field today? I hear that there's treasure hidden there.

In these pages I share some of the riches I have found in that field.

Your brother in Christ,

David Lee Martin

CHAPTER 1
FEROCIOUS MEN OF PRAYER

> *"What the Church needs to-day is not more machinery or better, not new organizations or more and novel methods, but men whom the Holy Ghost can use - men of prayer, men mighty in prayer."* — E.M. Bounds, *Power Through Prayer*

AS MEN of faith we surely declare that we want to see the will of God in operation. We have prayed more than once, *"Let Your will be done, let Your Kingdom come"*.

Are you ready and willing to become the answer to your own prayer?

God's will is clear, at least on one point:

> "I will therefore that men pray every where, lifting up holy hands, without wrath and doubting." (1 Timothy 2:8 KJV)

Your Father's will is that men should pray!

There has never been a time when such a call to spiritual arms has been more clear, and indeed more needed.

Like most men I struggle and often find my ferocious nature dissipated by the distractions and delusions of this present age. I am vaguely aware of the matrix I have allowed myself to be seduced by, but boy oh boy, how elusive the exit doorway seems to be in the unrelenting ebb and flow of everyday life.

And yet I also feel in my frailty and failing, a growing urgency to send out a call to any manly heart who will hear – it is TIME TO PRAY LIKE NEVER BEFORE!

FEROCITY AND FERVENCY

Manhood has an inherent nature that is ferocious. Savagely fierce and dangerous. Manhood pursues and subdues. It conquers and calls into being.

The devil and his minions want to shackle this Godlike power and do one of two things: tie it to purposes contrary to God and His Kingdom and let it run amok, devastating all that it touches, or conversely, castrate it so we find a church full of virtual eunuchs pretending to be 'nice' for a couple of short hours on a Sunday morning before reclaiming their manhood on Monday when they return to the office.

But the place the Almighty wants this aggressive winning nature to be truly harnessed is in the closet of prayer.

The devil fears nothing more than a man given to prayer.

As the famous preacher and revivalist, Robert Murray McCheyne said, "A holy man is a fearful weapon in the hands of a holy God."

When the men are praying the church is strong. When men fail in their duty the church languishes in powerless religion and man-centred philosophies and pursuits that meagrely scratch the surface of the world's crying need.

Fervency is a burning hot passion that spills into action. No true fire can remain tamed under the grave clothes – it has by its very nature to burst forth and consume. This is the quality of prayer that reaches the nostrils of Heaven!

> "The effective, fervent prayer of a righteous man avails much." (James 5:16 NKJV)

I want to be effective, and in order for that to happen the prayers that rise from my heart must be propelled by a burning desire. Fire causes the incense of the heart to ignite and stream heavenward. Feeble, fireless prayers are really not prayer at all. They may sound noble, and be eloquently crafted for the ears of men to applaud, but they will never avail like the untamed cries of a heart aflame with God's righteous cause.

Fervency is like a wildfire.

> "Then, like a wildfire, the Holy Spirit spread through their ranks..." (Acts 2:3 MSG)

Oh, how we need such a move of the Spirit in our ranks today!

How desperate the parched earth yearning for the rain of heaven! How the swollen belly of God's malnourished church rumbles for True Bread to satisfy its piteous cry for more.

PRAYER IS A HEART CRY

James 5:16 in the Amplified translation reads:

> "The earnest (heartfelt, continued) prayer of a righteous man makes tremendous power available [dynamic in its working]." (James 5:16 AMP)

Prayer is the voice of the heart. The deep calling unto deep. Men are called not to fill the air with pathetic half-hearted utterances and excuse themselves. No! No! No! Men are called to lend all the might of their being to this one essential work – to labor in the closet of prayer until the very foundations of the world shake with God's power and presence.

Is it any surprise that the world and the devil seek to keep men from this work?

Why is so much of the spiritual labour delegated to the women of the House?

Don't misunderstand me. I do not mean that in a derogatory way. A praying woman is equally as frightening as any man who has taken up his sword, but this is not written primarily to my sisters. It's written to you, dear brother!

The heavy lifting of prayer takes every shoulder

to bear it, but men have largely resigned their position as the bearers of the Ark and delighted themselves in carrying and building other things: reputations, businesses, wealth, education – all of these are replete with fervent men ploughing their blood and sweat into their establishment. But what of the closet?

Where are the warriors of faith willing to close themselves away until the flesh is utterly consumed and the spirit-man steps forth in glorious battle array?

Too few will hear I know, but even one can make a difference. History shows that one man and His God are a majority.

This call is not an easy one, nor without cost. It demands a depth of consecration and death to self far more than most are willing to pay, but the Holy Ghost stands on the threshold ushering us across the line.

It begins with a willingness. Not a wilfulness, for this savage territory we are entering is not won by the fire and fury of self. Instead, what is required is a yielding, putting aside "wrath and doubting," following the lead of the Holy Ghost as He takes the man and moulds him into a vessel of honour. A vessel through which He can lift up His best petitions.

Man of God, your search for significance has come to an end. Your seeking for purpose has found its prize. Prayer is your primary pursuit and glorious privilege.

Will you lean in and let Him lead you?

CHAPTER 2
FEROCIOUS
REALIZATION

*"Unless I had the spirit of prayer, I could do
nothing."* — *Charles Grandison Finney*

THE FEROCIOUS REALIZATION that Jesus
means what He says is one that radically changes
lives. The problem is, despite our lip service to the
same, we act out in ways that betray our true
standing concerning many of His more incendiary
statements.

One that strikes hard on the self-reliant nature of
ego-driven religious activity is found in John 15:5:

> *"...without me ye can do nothing."* (John
> 15:5 KJV)

As a church, and I speak very generally, the lack

of notable spiritual manifestation in our midst is only overshadowed by an equally shocking reliance on the methods of men. The Almighty, all-consuming, fearful, and fabulous God that we claim to worship conspicuously and consistently fails to attend our gatherings, and we in all our human glory step in and try to fill the gaps.

Instead of falling on our faces in abject poverty of spirit, lamenting our lack of any real power, we continue to frantically turn the handle of the man-centered machinery of ministry. It's as if we hold our hand up to the Holy Ghost and say, *"It's ok, Lord, we've got this!"* and carry on as if something is not desperately wrong. We close our eyes and ears to Jesus' warning, and if we are ever forced to face our nakedness, we flap our fig leaves ever harder; more activities, more and better programs, more concern for the comforts of the crowd that pays to keep the lights burning in our many buildings.

But where oh where is the light of God's glory?

Where are the signs and wonders? The notable, undeniable miracles of God at work among His people?

Should this stark and frightening disconnect between what we preach and hear week after week, and what we experience, not grip us with insatiable desperation for Truth and drive us to our knees?

CALLING THE MIGHTY MEN

I say again, this is not meant as a criticism, and most certainly not a slippery soapbox upon which I raise my stature above others and proclaim with the Pharisees that, *"I am not as other men" (Luke 18:11).*

No, I am the undone man beating his chest, crying loudly, *"God be merciful to me, for I am a sinner!" (Luke 18:13)*

It behooves us to remember daily that the prophet's finger can almost always point back at us, rightly declaring, *"You are that man!" (2 Samuel 12:7)*

I am the man who needs to pray more and better.

I am the man whose life is way too fond of the frivolities of this world.

I am the man whose dedication to the Saviour is found wanting on so many levels.

Yet there must also be a place to harness all of my meagre desire, what little fervency I possess, and join Gideon to cry out from the depths of the winepress;

> *"Oh my Lord, if the LORD be with us, why then is all this befallen us? and where be all his miracles which our fathers told us of, saying, Did not the LORD bring us up from Egypt? but now the LORD hath forsaken us,*

> *and delivered us into the hands of the (the*
> *enemy)." (Judges 6:13 KJV)*

Gideon was abundantly aware of his weakness. He prayed these prayers with his self-esteem even lower than the pit he was threshing in. The Scriptures tell us that Gideon was discovered in a winepress beating wheat, but really it was his confidence in God that had been thrashed more than any ear of corn.

And here is the kicker – the game changer for Gideon and for you and I - God's estimation of the trembling Gideon was entirely different.

> *"The angel of the LORD appeared unto him,*
> *and said unto him, The LORD is with thee,*
> *thou   mighty   man   of   valour."*
> *(Judges 6:12 KJV)*

Mighty man of valour? Looking around to make sure he was the only one there, Gideon immediately rejected God's ferocious words of affirmation.

But the trembling Israelite's protests of his inadequacy appear to have fallen on deaf ears.

His insistence that he was the least of the least, and that God must have surely mistaken him for someone else, was met by the assurance, *"Surely I will be with thee, and thou shalt smite the Midianites as one man... Go in this thy might..." (Judges 6:16;14 KJV)*

And so it is with us.

Our passion and prayers may seem insipid in the face of the vast needs that we face, but they are in reality mighty for the pulling down of strongholds.

It is not our power but His that is called upon and released when we forsake our meagre methodologies and return to the Biblical pattern of fervent, unceasing prayer.

I believe that God is visiting men in their bunkers of fear and failure today, pulling them up, dusting them down, and placing the mighty sword of prayer in their hands. Bloodied and weak we may be from decades of dry religion and worldly domination, but Heaven is not measuring us by the rule of this age. Papa is not laying the harsh rod of performance upon his people.

God is calling men of all manner to the mighty work of intercession.

Through prayer, men are changed from glory to glory and lunge from faith to faith. The passing and pointless pursuits of the age give way to eternal purposes.

Cold, unbelieving hearts are awakened again to their inheritance and identity.

It all begins with a ferocious and absolute

realisation that nothing we can do in our own earthly strength can ever accomplish heavenly results.

That's why prayer is the urgent necessity to which we must yield. Prayer is the priority that must oust every other effort.

In doing so, and when the men of God's house rise to humble their hearts and lift their voices to the One through whom all things are possible, we take our first long-awaited steps toward revival fires that will blaze through the barricades.

History will tell of the company of men who rose from their stupor and obtained the promise of reformation in this generation. The books of remembrance in heaven will be filled with their exploits in the spirit.

Mighty man of valour! Hear the call. The arena of your victory will be the unseen realm that pulls the strings of the world below.

God is not looking for more actors on the stage, or even preachers in the pulpit. He is looking for men who are willing to stand in the gap.

> *"And I sought for a man among them, that should make up the hedge, and stand in the gap before me for the land, that I should not destroy it…" (Ezekiel 22:30 KJV)*

This verse tragically ends with the words, *"...but I found none."*

Oh, dear Father, let this not be the testimony of our generation. Raise up men of prayer! Scour the pits of discouragement and disillusionment and reignite a vision of all that's possible if we follow hard after You.

Arise, oh God, in all your might, and scatter your enemies!

CHAPTER 3
GOD'S CHOICE MEN

"There is power in prayer. When men work,
they work. But when men pray, God
works!" — Angus Buchan

THE FIERY GOD we serve does not measure suitability for service as men do.

His choicest vessels and mightiest warriors are not the ones who grace the magazine covers or sport spandex outfits to marvel the world with their outlandish exploits. Such heroes are figments of entertainment, but powerless to contend with the real evils the universe is facing.

What we need today is not another Captain or Iron Man, we need those who know the real and only Captain, Jesus Christ - the one with eyes like fire and feet like burnished brass!

In His Word God gives insight to His methods.

It is not the popular or the professional who stand in His courts, nor those considered mighty in the eyes of the world. Such have hearts that are hard to break open.

Instead, those who come to Him are like the mighty ones of David:

> "David therefore departed thence, and escaped to the cave Adullam: and when his brethren and all his father's house heard it, they went down thither to him. And every one that was in distress, and every one that was in debt, and every one that was discontented, gathered themselves unto him; and he became a captain over them: and there were with him about four hundred men." (1 Samuel 22:1–2 KJV)

Four hundred distressed, discontented, debtors became the heroic heralds of the king.

God's call to His unlikely tribe continues today…

> "For ye see your calling, brethren, how that not many wise men after the flesh, not

many mighty, not many noble, are called: But God hath chosen the foolish things of the world to confound the wise; and God hath chosen the weak things of the world to confound the things which are mighty; And base things of the world, and things which are despised, hath God chosen, yea, and things which are not, to bring to nought things that are: That no flesh should glory in his presence." (1 Corinthians 1:26–29 KJV)

Humility comes at a high price for most of us. We have tasted the bitter humiliation of failure. We have stood wondering who we are, and why we were born.

Life has bruised our ego and delivered challenges that at times threatened to crush us. But from these flames, and in the hot coals of suffering, true and tested manhood has been formed.

His call is to you now, man of God.

The world may have written you off, but God has contended for your place in His courts. Whatever shame you carry, whatever past failures you are weighed by, the Captain of your soul has sliced them from your back. He endured the ravages of the cross, taking the punishments that your foolhardy actions deserved, and bore the shame the devil would like to bury you with.

Thank God it was buried with Christ instead!

Now, surrounded as a runner in a race we are guaranteed to win, Adullam's arch warriors are laying aside all that anchors them to the world, and rising to take their place in the heavenlies. Our eyes are fixed on the One who slain the hordes that stood against us.

> "Wherefore seeing we also are compassed about with so great a cloud of witnesses, let us lay aside every weight, and the sin which doth so easily beset us, and let us run with patience the race that is set before us, Looking unto Jesus the author and finisher of our faith" (Hebrews 12:1–2 KJV)

Dear brother, there is a place set for you in the heavens. A seat of authority bearing you name.

You have been *raised up together, and made to sit together in heavenly places in Christ Jesus:" (Ephesians 2:6 KJV)*

From here your new authority will be exercised. It is the authority wielded only by those who have learned to hold the hilt of prayer.

Like Eleazar in 2 Samuel 23 our hands cleave to the sword of prayer. God's Word on your lips has become the steel through which God works great victories.

Not by might, not by power, but by the Spirit of the Lord who lives within you.

CHAPTER 4
THAT KIND OF MAN

*"I am not waiting for a move of God, I am a
move of God!"* — *William Booth*

FIERCE MEN ARE few and far between. Men
who have faced their demons and slain their fears.
Men who have taken a stand on the inside and said,
"No more!" to the crippling castrations of the
status quo.

How can a man ever flourish whilst playing the
role of "Mr. nice guy"?

Call him what you will, "Mr. church guy", "Mr.
Business man", "Mr. plumber, baker, candlestick
maker..."

The man himself lost under labels. Screaming to
break free and shout his reality.

Men of Adullam, looking for the King to come. You know who you are!

We have already introduced the motley clay pots God chooses for His greatest works.

Distressed, discontented, and wanting. Beyond caring what others think or say. Desperate for change. The descriptions of these men who discovered themselves in the cave sing a different tune to the one we usually hear. These were the mighty ones in the making.

No longer hiding under a blanket of respectability they gathered to discover a new way of living.

These are the ones ready to embark on exploits worthy of the telling.

These are men who venture willingly into places of danger. The place of prayer has been painted as a paradise, but often we find blood on the field.

Beside the still waters the ignorant ones who were not trained to spot the prowling lion lie bleeding.

The peaceful waters and the table that's prepared is set in the presence of enemies that are very real, and very intent upon the destruction of all you hold dear.

In this age, our stance and outfit for the meal is one that resembles heavy armour, not smart casual or evening wear.

The two lionlike Moabites, fear and unbelief,

want to back you off. Political correctness cheers their efforts, but Adullamites are deaf to their accusations and intimidation.

> 66 "Benaiah... slew two lionlike men of Moab: he went down also and slew a lion in a pit in a snowy day." (1 Chronicles 11:22 KJV)

Are you man who will wrestle your detractors to the ground?

Will you leap into the prayer pit and slay the beast? The weather is raging, the winds are blowing contrary. The danger is real, present and salivating for your demise.

Did Benaiah run in the opposite direction? Did he shy from the battle?

No, he chose to jump into the pit and face the fight. He "went down" so he could emerge a better man.

I want to be a man who jumps into the pit. Who doesn't cover-up, gloss over, pretend or parade. I want to be a man with blood on his sword from the battles I have fought and won. With myself. With my own lies and layers.

It takes courage to step out of this world's broken system knowing that living the warrior's way is not a matter of right and wrong, it is a matter of personal character. My choice to lie is a matter of character. My choice to tell the truth is a matter of character. My decision to live in line with the Word of God and not my passing fancies is a matter of character.

If I respect myself I will tell the truth. If I respect others I will tell them the truth.

How often do we support one another's fantasies by agreeing with things that are clearly not working. Will I climb behind the bushes and fig trees of society's norms and stay hidden in my stories?

Will I continue to insist that the emperor is fully clothed and all is well?

Behind the lie, the prowling lion of discontent taunts the people of God with feelings of inadequacy.

The growling rumble of "never enough".

I can kid myself and say I'm content with my life in God, and that the spiritual temperature of the nations is rising, but it would not be true.

A great chill has overtaken the church. The frosty hand of materialism has frozen its assets.

Leonard Ravenhill said of the church, *"People say the church today is 'growing and expanding.' Yes, it's ten miles wide now—and about a quarter-inch deep."*

The world needs more than just 'good' men.

There's a vast gulf between a "good" man and a

"mighty" man. I know which side of the valley I want to stand on.

A Good dad? I don't want to be a "good" dad. I want to be a great dad who is 100% invested in my sons and daughters. A man who impacts my posterity so deeply by example they would never want to depart from the way of truth. Ever.

I can continue to wrap myself in kid-glove fantasies that I'm the husband I need to be for my queen, but who am I kidding? Years of excuses and not turning up as the man I need to be leaves its mark.

Am I the faithful follower of Jesus I claim to be? When it suits me, yes. But the hard sayings and tough meat of His Way stick in my comfortable throat. I still find myself choking on the facts of my own pitiful lack of dedication to sell all and follow Him to the edge - to leap from the cliff edge of philosophy and religious observance into a real and raw life of honest faith. And don't lay the charismatic card on me. Just because you speak in tongues and raise your hands doesn't cut it in a pit on a snowy day!

I no longer want to defend my lions. I can't leave them prowling my pits and the caverns of my soul.

What will happen when I stand before my King and give account? Will I be faced with the man I could have been, or will I stand with the scars of a life well lived?

66 "...he   went   down"   (1   Chronicles 11:22 KJV)

This guy chose to wrestle his lions. He didn't wait until it was convenient. He didn't hang around for favourable circumstances when it was appropriate and acceptable to do so.

He chose to go down into the dark places with his sword unsheathed.

I want to be that kind of man.

The nutcase who goes down into the pit in a snowy day to slay his lions.

How about you?

CHAPTER 5
FEROCIOUS REPENTANCE

"You can't live wrong and pray right."
— *Leonard Ravenhill*

A FIERCE LOVE following hard after God will always be attended by an equally ferocious hatred for sin.

The doctrine of free grace has been watered down by the modern western church to a fluffy teaching that turns a blind eye to sin and excuses the sinner without any requirement to change.

While I wholeheartedly agree that the broad boundaries of grace are far beyond anything we could reasonably expect or imagine, the Scriptures nowhere teach that sin is acceptable within or outside the church.

The message of the kingdom does not begin with

the word believe. The starting point is a line in the sand called "repent".

"Repent, and believe the gospel."

Go, and sin no more!

Without holiness no man will see the Lord *(Hebrews 12:14)*.

If we want to see God move in the manner we desire it will undoubtedly require a depth of consecration to His purposes and His Person that burns the chaff from our lives in a most uncomfortable way.

Repentance is not a message often preached nowadays. Being faced with our lukewarmness, challenged to not only applaud Jesus but lay down our life for Him, is not one that readily fits with our manic me-centered society.

Paul wrote:

66   *"Ye have not yet resisted unto blood, striving against sin." (Hebrews 12:4 KJV)*

This suggests a stringent and aggressive dealing with the besetting habits of the old life, and a ferocious taking hold of the new.

Many old saints speak of praying through with great heartbreaking supplication to a definite experience of sanctification. Like other watershed moments in their walk with God they speak of a defining moment where Christ so took hold of their heart that the very power of sin was utterly vanquished in their life.

For most of us, and I am the chief, the penalty of sin has been majestically and finally declared void through the precious blood of Jesus, but we still struggle with the power that sin sometimes exerts over our flesh. I believe that both sin's penalty and power were taken care of at the cross, but it is for us to take hold with fervency if we want to live in the reality of this Truth.

Instead, men often prefer to live in the realms of empty confession. It is one thing to say, "I am holy." It is quite another to live holy. Yes, indeed, righteousness is accounted to us through the sacrificial substitution of Christ, but dear brothers, the legal standing we now enjoy must bud and blossom into a radically distinct life of difference. Christian men are not supposed to blend in. Our very lives should be a reproach to the ways of the world around us, and to any half-hearted bloodless christianity (small 'c').

At heart repentance is a call to close communion with God.

> *"Or despisest thou the riches of his goodness and forbearance and longsuffering; not knowing that the goodness of God leadeth thee to repentance?" (Romans 2:4 KJV)*

The grace and goodness of our God invites us to turn away from sin, not continue in an endless cycle of *sin > guilt > repent > sin > guilt > repent ad infinitum.*

The process, if repentance is deep and genuine will be *sin > repent.* Period.

FIERCE MEN HOLD THEMSELVES TO ACCOUNT

If we genuinely want to see the world turn to God, surely we should be turning first.

How can we call others to forsake the world if we ourselves are still in bed with it?

How can we reprove the adultery of the masses, if the church is still courting whorish affections for this present age and its attractions?

Regardless of what others may think or the doctrines they throw in your face to convince you that comfortable, cross-less Christianity is acceptable to our Father, never relent in your pursuit of purity.

I believe at the deepest level repentance is required in the core of our being. Our first steps into the Kingdom are afforded through repentance and faith, but as we walk forward the requirement on our manhood increases.

A baby might soil the carpet without reproach, but a full grown man in a diaper is shameful.

Our great Father is not only our Comforter, He is our Corrector and our Chastiser.

The following portion of Scripture is worthy of a full reading:

> "And ye have forgotten the exhortation which speaketh unto you as unto children, My son, despise not thou the chastening of the Lord, nor faint when thou art rebuked of him: For whom the Lord loveth he chasteneth, and scourgeth every son whom he receiveth. If ye endure chastening, God dealeth with you as with sons; for what son is he whom the father chasteneth not? But if ye be without chastisement, whereof all are partakers, then are ye bastards, and not sons. Furthermore we have had fathers of our flesh which corrected us, and we gave them reverence: shall we not much rather be in subjection unto the Father of spirits, and live? For they verily for a few days chastened us after their own

pleasure; but he for our profit, that we might be partakers of his holiness. Now no chastening for the present seemeth to be joyous, but grievous: nevertheless afterward it yieldeth the peaceable fruit of righteousness unto them which are exercised thereby." (Hebrews 12:5–11 KJV)

A full son in the house will be trained by the Master. His heavy hand of correction will purge every son so they might bear more fruit.

I personally invite the Spirit of repentance to search my heart.

> "Search me, O God, and know my heart: try me, and know my thoughts: And see if there be any wicked way in me, and lead me in the way everlasting." (Psalm 139:23–24 KJV)

I do not want to carry contraband into the Kingdom life I seek to live. How sad it is when hidden sin is brought to light for all the world to see.

Before public exposure is necessary, how much better to fall on our faces privately, and allow Him to deal with our prideful and presumptuous ways.

Do you think Daddy really likes our parades and pretences? Will we not all one day stand before the One whose eyes search all things? Will our works and the motives that prompted them not be tried by fire?

This, friend, is a day of preparation, and repentance is not optional. Jesus did not suggest repent *OR* believe. He commanded repent *AND* believe.

Every significant move of God through the centuries has been marked by a deep undoing of God's people first, and then a glorious decent of God's conviction upon the world.

Let's not wait until God corners us in the shining light of his fearful glory before we hang our shame on the cross and pass to a new and cleaner life.

Do it now!

Take your compromises, your competitiveness, your critical spirit, your filthy tongue, and unbelieving heart, and lay them honestly before the only One who can sweep them away and usher in a new creation.

Like a crawling bug breaking from the limits of its cocoon and taking colorful flight, rise to your metamorphosis.

A new and fully formed man in Christ Jesus!

CHAPTER 6
THE SAVAGERY OF SIN

*"The individual who truly repents, not only
sees sin to be detestable and vile and
worthy of abhorrence, but he really
abhors it, and hates it in his heart. A
person may see sin to be hurtful and
abominable, while yet his heart loves it,
and desires it, and clings to it. But
when he truly repents, he most heartily
abhors and renounces it."* — Charles
Finney

WHEN MEN LOOKED at his body on the cross it
was said he no longer resembled a human being. So
ravaged, savagely torn, so bruised and shredded, so
bloodied and mauled – more a carcass than a king.
Christ, the sacrifice.

Even those who called for his crucifixion were horrified at what they saw.

> 66 "…everyone was appalled. He didn't even look human— a ruined face, disfigured past recognition." (Isaiah 52:14 MESSAGE)

And yet, what are we witnessing?

What is it that we are looking upon when our eyes burn to behold such brutal inhumanity? How cold, unfeeling, careless and calculated the hands and hearts that devised such torture? What crime could deserve such unspeakable punishment?

Have you for a second seen Him? Have you looked upon the One who willingly took your sin?

Has *"Jesus Christ been evidently set forth, crucified among you?" (Galatians 3:1 KJV)*

Have your tears poured buckets when you drink in the terror?

Set Christ crucified evidently before my eyes became my prayer for several weeks. I wanted, like the Galatians, to appreciate more the price paid for my freedom.

THEN I SAW HIM, AND IT WAS ME...

Then I looked and saw. Evidently, before me. The man, if he can be called such, nailed to the cross. But it was not the form that struck fear in my heart, it was what happened next. My chest tore open wide in gaping wound, and spilling forth like black stinking tar my sins spewed out like an obscene river. The stench. The horror. The concentrated, thick, sticky, stream of filth – a witches brew of pride and lust, love of money and affection for the world's lies and licentiousness. Lukewarmness, envy, adultery, shamefaced lying and conniving. It was all here. No religious fig leaf could ever cover the terror tumbling from my hidden man.

And more…

Like a black hole irresistibly sucking all that comes close into its swirling darkness – Jesus Christ on the cross siphoning my sin into his very own being. Relentlessly and selflessly taking it all into himself. Becoming sin before my eyes.

That is why the cross is so horrifying.

All were appalled at what they saw there, but what they saw with their natural eyes is nothing compared to what was happening in the spirit.

THE SAVAGERY OF SIN

Have you ever looked upon your sin with the same disgust as the eyes that beheld the Saviour that day? Blood dripping from every orifice? Savage gouges weeping blood from the scourging? Pierced holes dropping his perfect life into the dust?

Friend, the picture of Christ on the cross, evidently set forth in the gospels, is a picture of the savagery of sin. When we dare to gaze upon Him, we see ourselves without Him. We look upon the horror not just of a man so tortured and twisted, but the twisted nature of our heart apart from him, the torture of a soul bound for hell if no daysman can be found.

My sin nailed him there.

It was the heartless, murderous nature of my iniquity that sliced and whipped him raw.

Sin has no other aim but your death and mine.

Sin's mandate is your destruction.

Yet we fail so often to see through sin's disguise.

Parading in coquettish familiarity with the leanings of our flesh, the lusts of our eyes, of the flesh, the pride of life, all offer themselves daily to our appetites, smeared in makeup and cheap perfume. Promising delight but delivering death they entice good men to forsake their conscience and count the blood of Christ a common thing.

And once the deed is done, the thought received, the graceless word spoken, the gluttonous appetite satisfied, the harlot strips her cloak away and dons the garb of judge and jury, condemning our compromise and berating our weakness.

One minute shameless enticement to sin, the next shameful condemnation, and we join the jury in agreement. Shame beats down upon us in a thousand tearful sorrows and promises of tomorrows fidelity.

How much more the shame of one who never sinned? How must the Saviour have turned from the prospect, disgusted by the very thought of his soul being invaded?

Can we ever comprehend the blood that broke from Jesus' brow as he contemplated the horror of sin upon himself? He became sin. The sinless, spotless, pure Son of God.

How great the price that he paid so personally for you!

Could we ever really imagine the true cost that was paid that night in Gethsemane? On the cross at Calvary.

Do we for a moment grasp why the Father had to turn his eyes away? The One who sees all, blinded by the horror of our sins and demon lovers savaging His Son.

Grace is offered freely to the sinner.

But it is far from free.

A full and fearful price was paid.

How will you respond?

Will pornography rob your place at the table?

Will dishonest practices to save a cent on the dollar in taxes sabotage securing your rich inheritance in the heavens?

Will adulterous flirting with the world mar your marriage to the purposes of God?

What appear to be inconsequential compromises here on earth, severely undermine your integrity and authority in the arena of prayer and spiritual warfare.

DON'T BE A SECOND HAND MAN

The story of the sons of Sceva in Acts 19 is eye-opening. Addressing evil spirits with second-hand knowledge doesn't work:

> "And the evil spirit answered and said, Jesus I know, and Paul I know; but who are ye?" (Acts 19:15 KJV)

As men of God we cannot piggyback on the

pulpit preachers we faithfully listen to every week. The gospel that we preach must show up 24/7 in the way we live.

Holiness is not an option, it's a necessity if you want to operate in spiritual authority.

Paul so clearly spoke of dealing with your own baggage before presuming that you can effectively deal with demons:

> "For though we walk in the flesh, we do not war after the flesh: (For the weapons of our warfare *are* not carnal, but mighty through God to the pulling down of strong holds;) Casting down imaginations, and every high thing that exalteth itself against the knowledge of God, and bringing into captivity every thought to the obedience of Christ; And having in a readiness to revenge all disobedience, when your obedience is fulfilled." (2 Corinthians 10:3–6 KJV)

As Henry Ward Beecher said:

> "It is not well for a man to pray cream and live skim milk."

In some meetings I have attended, I have heard proclamations binding "every evil spirit" over a city or nation, demanding that ancient spirits be dislodged in an instant, or that swathes of dark humanity spill into the Kingdom.

Is the name of Jesus, and faith in that name, enough to affect such world-changing effects? Doubtless it is. Every knee will one day bow to the matchless name of our King. But only lives perfectly aligned with the name they proclaim can anticipate full manifestation of its authority in the spiritual realm.

Prayer is so much more than just words. In fact the most powerful prayers are unutterable, undergirded by a heart fully and completely yielded to the One they proclaim.

As much as I wish it were as simple as binding every contrary spirit, and calling the lost like moths to a flame, the iceberg under the waterline doesn't carry the kind of weight required for this universal displacement.

A depth of acquaintance with God, a foundation of moment by moment obedience, and an unswerving yielding to the Holy Ghost, is the ground upon which authority is exercised.

Our character has to line up with our lips. Such authority does not come without price, and presumptuous prayers often do more damage than good.

Ferocity doesn't show up in prideful outward flames berating the world for its ills, or boorish berating of devils, it is evidenced in heartrending repentance behind the private doors of the homes of real men who mean business with the Holy One of Israel.

If your religion is just an outer garment you'll end up like the Sceva boys, overcome, reeling from the battles you engage in, naked and wounded. An object of derision for the devil.

Let's be men who know how to face our failings with valour by putting our faces to the floor and seeking the Sanctifier with absolute humility of heart.

A man with nothing left to hide is powerful indeed!

CHAPTER 7
SOME MEN TRUST IN HORSES

"Are you destitute for the Fire of God? Nothing else matters! Possess ye God's Fire! All else is void!" — Dr. Pazaria Smith

> "Some *trust* in chariots, and some in horses: but we will remember the name of the LORD our God." (Psalm 20:7 KJV)

THE TEMPTATION TO trust in our own wisdom and strength is ever present. God made man in His own image, and we are godlike in our ambitions and ability to envisage and create.

Harnessing horsepower; more effort, greater influence, stronger, better, bigger methods, means we often produce just enough results to pacify our ego.

Like a fast food meal our hunger is staved for a moment with no real gain.

A flabby self-satisfied church is a reproach, repulsive to the world.

Caught in the numbers game. Bottom line living. Counting beans. Measuring ourselves by ourselves. Foolishness!

> "For we dare not make ourselves of the number, or compare ourselves with some that commend themselves: but they measuring themselves by themselves, and comparing themselves among themselves, are not wise." (2 Corinthians 10:12 KJV)

The need in our day is more than a meeting. Endless rallies and revival conferences are an invisible drop in an ocean of pain, seeking to bring people *to* church instead of *being* the church that goes to the people.

And go we must, but not before we are formed and filled with fire.

First the call to be with Him, then the power to go.

> "And he ordained twelve, that they should be with him, and that he might

send them forth to preach." (Mark 3:14 KJV)

It is in the presence of Jesus that we will be empowered to accomplish His commission.

Moses understood this when he pleaded:

> "And Moses said to the Lord, If Your Presence does not go with me, do not carry us up from here! For by what shall it be known that I and Your people have found favor in Your sight? Is it not in Your going with us so that we are distinguished, I and Your people, from all the other people upon the face of the earth?" (Exodus 33:15–16 AMP)

Even those who had spent three years stapled to the Saviour's side, performed miracles in His name, and fed multitudes with just a few crumbs, were told, "Don't go until…"

Until what?

Our tendency to run, to mount the horse and charge, might mean we gallop with sincere intention in completely the wrong direction.

66 *"Being assembled together with them, Jesus commanded them that they should not depart from Jerusalem, but wait for the promise of the Father, which, saith he, ye have heard of me. For John truly baptized with water; but ye shall be baptized with the Holy Ghost not many days hence." (Acts 1:4–5 KJV)*

In the words of E M Bounds:

66 "What the Church needs today is not more machinery or better, not new organizations or more and novel methods, but men whom the Holy Ghost can use -- men of prayer, men mighty in prayer. The Holy Ghost does not flow through methods, but through men. He does not come on machinery, but on men. He does not anoint plans, but men - men of prayer."

True when it was written and true today.

All of our efforts are vain when naked of anointing.

There is no greater need that the church has today than the need for God's might power to flow. The strongest push in human flesh is laughable. The devil doubles up in derision and delight when he witnesses our fleshly displays, but once the weighty *kabod* glory of the Holy Ghost clothes God's people demons tremble.

Oh that our generation would experience the nation shakings we read of in times past. That the prayer stock of previous saintly men would be cashed in and added to our own, purchasing from Heaven a fresh move that ushers in the second coming of our King.

For all of our going, riding gospel horses across the lands, the darkness yet prevails. We need a new equipping. Fresh fire from Heaven to consume our prideful self-reliance.

I mean no offence to those whose lives are poured into any enterprise designed to bring Jesus to the masses. My prayers are that every ounce of sweat will bear a thousandfold return but my heart yearns for something no man can give.

Jesus said this of the dramatic work of salvation, especially of the self-reliant:

"With men it is impossible, but not with God: for with God all things are possible." (Mark 10:27 KJV)

My suspicion is if we were to observe the horsing

around in most houses of worship each week, we'd come away having experienced pretty much exclusively *"with men it is possible."*

Every part of the carefully orchestrated experience from the hello at the door to the final blessing could all have happened without a lick of assistance from Heaven.

As I say, I am not pointing fingers, not criticising men's best efforts to serve, not shaming the pastorate for the paltry presence and thin sermonising thousands endure week after week.

I am just pointing to the one thing needful. The one thing missing. The one thing necessary for mission to become the natural overflow from the House of God.

The Holy Ghost!

He alone can make Heaven's purpose real to the hearts of our generation. He and only He has the power to convict an aching world of sin, righteousness, and judgement.

As at the first the method of Heaven has never changed.

> *"These all continued with one accord in prayer and supplication,"* *(Acts 1:14 NKJV)*

They waiting with one request and expectation,

knowing that their commission to bear spiritual children was castrated without the answer.

The Promise of the Father *(Luke 24:49)* was their one accord.

Today the divisions and debates over what is needed to see the long overdue breakthrough and stem the tide of evil in our culture multiply like rabbits on viagra. One insists seeker friendly, another the addition of social action. Some advocate strict holiness in clothing and conduct, others a liberal theology that embraces all manner of human debauchery in the name of love and acceptance.

The voice of God's house is splintered, diluted in an ocean of opinions.

Trotting from one trend to the next, the command to tarry remains unheeded.

Heaven's mandate is simple:

Tarry until ye be endued with power.

Then go forth in the strength of thousand horsemen, riding heavenly chariots roughshod over the plans of satan and his cohorts.

There is one call and one alone sufficient for our need - a call to prayer that we might secure once again an outpouring of the Holy Ghost in our dry and desperate day.

CHAPTER 8
FEROCIOUS PURSUIT

*"There are parts of our calling, works of the
Holy Spirit, and defeats of the darkness
that will come no other way than
through furious, fervent, faith-filled,
unceasing prayer."* — Beth Moore

PEOPLE CHASE A LOT OF THINGS. The planet seems to be filled with people running everywhere, hurrying to who knows what. If you ask people what they are running to obtain I venture that many would not even be able to give you an answer.

But one pursuit is certain in its rewards.

Jesus made it clear that all our chasing will only result in us catching our own greedy tail if we have our priorities mixed up.

> "*But seek ye first the kingdom of God, and his righteousness; and all these things shall be added unto you.*" (Matthew 6:33 KJV)

All these 'things' that swallow our time and attention are already prepped on a platter for those who will seek first and make their prime objective the possession of God's Kingdom.

The desperate need today is not for men to make more money or build better and bigger houses. The cry of the earth is not for a multiplication of polished pulpits and slicker more streamlined programs.

The groaning of the world is for men who know how to secure moves of God's Spirit. That rare breed who have so taken hold of Heaven that their prayers bring the realms of God down among people. It has ever been so and ever will until Jesus returns.

How many have forsaken all to follow their Saviour? How many have sold their fields to buy the precious pearl? Is this radical renunciation of all that takes us away from our first love not the price that Papa calls for among His chosen?

Evangelist D. L. Moody said

> "The world has yet to see what God can do with a man fully consecrated to him. By God's help, I aim to be that man."

Dear friend, there is no moment lost in vain that is spent in pursuit of God. All of our fruitless striving for reputation and recognition in this world is dust on the wind compared to the inestimable riches we store up in Heaven through hours poured into secret prayer. The world, and perhaps even more sadly the church, may mock what they consider 'wasted' time in the closet, but their eyes do not see the true riches that reside there.

THE PURPOSE OF HEAVEN – A NEW PENTECOST

You are being prepared for eternity, and that glorious realm of God is the natural habitat for your born-again spirit. The Father is calling you to His side to share in His Kingdom purposes. It may be foolishness to man's reasonable mind, and a reproach to the flesh, but prayer is the highest call any man can attain to. It is the very expression of the Saviour through the hearts of His people.

I urge you to read accounts of revival through the generations to grasp the truth of what I'm saying. Without exception, prayer, fervent heartfelt insistent prayer that wrestles for the blessing, has been responsible for the earth's greatest seasons of divine visitation.

Of course we have to act. Indeed the gospel must

be preached. Prayer alone is not an end in itself. But it is the beginning!

Too often men make their plans and tag prayer to the tail asking for God's stamp of approval on their genius. Concoctions of reason, skill and gifting come first, followed by brief requests for the Father's hand to rest upon them.

God's method, at least the one we see in the life of the Saviour, and in every chapter of the Book of Acts, turns this philosophy on its head. Pray first. Then act.

John G Lake, a man used mightily of God in the early 1900's, received an angelic visitation in response to the hungry cry of his heart. The angel took Lake's Bible and opened to the book of Acts. He pointed to the outpouring of the Holy Spirit on the day of Pentecost, and then proceeded through the book highlighting the outstanding emphasis on the power and presence of the Holy Ghost throughout.

The angel then spoke these words:

> "This is Pentecost as God gave it through the heart of Jesus. Strive for this. Contend for this. Teach the people to pray for this. For this, and this alone, will meet the necessity of the human heart, and this alone will have the power to overcome the

forces of darkness. Pray. Pray. Pray. Teach the people to pray. Prayer and prayer alone, much prayer, persistent prayer, is the door of entrance into the heart of God. "

This Pentecostal blessing and power alone can meet the necessity of the human heart. No man-made religion, however well-intentioned and sincere, can ever overcome the forces of darkness.

Nothing but a ferocious pursuit that shuns all else will be sufficient to break through.

But...but...but...

I already hear the procession of necessities busily excusing us from the call.

God's promise has leveled all such objections.

"Seek first the Kingdom of God..." – our responsibility.

"...and all these things will be added." God's response.

Do we dare believe Him and radically prioritize prayer? Are you ready to hitch your prosperous hopes to this prayerful purpose, believing God for favourable outcomes?

Are you ready to turn the level up on your ferocious pursuit of Heaven's blessing? Every day dedicated to securing such a move will be abundantly rewarded here and in eternity. Many of the richest reputations in heaven are being earned in obscurity here on earth even as we speak.

CHAPTER 9
YOUR GENTLENESS HAS MADE ME GREAT

"To desire revival... and at the same time to
neglect (personal) prayer and devotion
is to wish one way and walk
another." — A.W. Tozer

TWICE THE SCRIPTURES record the words of David, "Thou hast also given me the shield of thy salvation: and thy gentleness hath made me great." *(2 Samuel 22:36; Psalm 18:35).*

Here we have a warrior of the highest calibre, a true man after God's own heart and fierce to the core in devotion, worship, and war, yet when describing what empowered him to reign in life he chose this defining feature of God's personality above all others - gentleness.

When we speak of fierce it's easy to slip into the

natural and picture belligerent nature loudly barging around in the spiritual realm insisting on its own way. Such a picture is comical indeed. Instead, the truly fierce man of God will be marked by humility and a gentle spirit. He will understand his place and exercise his authority accordingly.

Being in the presence of God for prolonged periods is transformative. We look long upon the nature and personality of Christ, and the same Spirit that He carried works that nature into us as His ambassadors.

66 "But we all, with open face beholding as in a glass the glory of the Lord, are changed into the same image from glory to glory, even as by the Spirit of the Lord." (2 Corinthians 3:18 KJV)

The meek, not the mouthy, inherit the earth.

Meekness describes manly strength harnessed and held in subjection to the purposes of God. An abiding resolute authority that is unmoved by criticism and unconcerned about the fickle attitudes of others. Far from the hothead who reacts to contrary circumstances with untempered emotion, the fierce man of God is held in holy balance, never tipped from his place of authority and peace.

Gentleness, meekness, kindness, goodness, and love, are the laws that work in the members of the true man of God. While the world's fierce "men" are comical parodies of manhood, rippling with steroid induced brutality, men of the sanctuary are muscled inwardly and out - their strength is not just wrapped around a dying frame, they are renewed each day in the presence of God.

> "For which cause we faint not; but though our outward man perish, yet the inward man is renewed day by day." (2 Corinthians 4:16 KJV)

As you learn to pray and contend with vigour in the spiritual realm, the contrary spirits that have been assigned to arrest your progress will be the unlikely sparring partners that help shape a holy character and dependance on God to fight wisely and successfully. This vital connection to God, much like the supply lines so needful in war, will drive you deeper and deeper into His nature.

Men will marvel at your love and grace while demons tremble at your warring, winning, unwaning resistance to their lies and schemes.

The signs of spiritual strength and connection show up in fruits of character.

> "...the fruit of the Spirit is love, joy, peace, longsuffering, gentleness, goodness, faith, meekness, temperance: against such there is no law. And they that are Christ's have crucified the flesh with the affections and lusts." (Galatians 5:22–24 KJV)

What the world lampoons as weakness, men of fierce prayer recognise as principles against which no other spiritual law can prevail.

Jesus taught and demonstrated that we overcome evil with good, hate with love, greed with generosity, and crush doubt and unbelief with fearless faith.

These are weapons that are woven into the Christlike nature of men who love the Sanctuary. Wield them well, my brother. Love outrageously. Pray passionately. Heap coals on the heads of your enemies, feeding your detractors so the demons that drive them crumble in confusion.

The stronger your hand becomes in the spiritual realm, the gentler and more harnessed by grace it will be here on earth.

CHAPTER 10
HIS NAME, THROUGH FAITH IN HIS NAME, HAS MADE THIS MAN STRONG

"Great names come and go, but the name of Jesus remains. The devil still hates it, the world still opposes it, but God still blesses it and we can still claim it! "In the name of Jesus" is the key that unlocks the door of prayer and the treasury of God's grace." — Warren W. Wiersbe

ONE OF THE hindrances to prayer is the idea that the strength of your petitions rests upon your own power or holiness. Not discounting the progressive work of sanctification that is at work in your spirit, the truth remains that our efficacy in spiritual things is based solely upon the finished work of Christ.

His perfect work, not our perfect conduct, is the bedrock of confidence in the closet.

The devil will come, marvelling that a feeble and fallible vessel like you could presume to make a difference.

Satan, being the self-obsessed narcissist that he is, will try and do what he does best and get you to turn your gaze from Jesus and look to yourself. In the garden he tried to convince Adam and Eve that they could operate apart from God. "Self" is his stock-in-trade. He still uses that scheme to great effect.

You are a god he lauds. You need no-one and your efforts and ego are magnificent and worthy of enthronement.

Or perhaps, when it suits his sulphurous purpose, he'll pop the balloon of self-inflation and convince you that you're a worse than a worm, disqualified on the basis of your miserable unforgivable failings.

You have not earned the right to pray powerfully he'll contend.

You don't deserve an audience with the Almighty.

You are not holy, pure, wise, or powerful enough to make a difference.

The gospel still befuddles the dark mind of the flesh, none more than the defeated demons who failed to see the wisdom of God at work through the cross. Law draws its vitality from the passing life of the flesh, and delivers only death to its proponents. Satan is indeed a legalist.

The irony is that he failed to see the legal landslide Heaven was about to win when he laid his most vicious blows on the Son of God.

> "Which none of the princes of this world knew: for had they known it, they would not have crucified the Lord of glory." (1 Corinthians 2:8 KJV)

What satan thought his greatest victory actually became his downfall and ultimate demise!

The cross changes everything. On that bloody stake your old self died and a new man arose. In Christ it is no longer your own holiness that counts, but His. In Him you became the righteousness of God.

As Peter pointed out to those who sought is exaltation:

> "Ye men of Israel, why marvel ye at this? or why look ye so earnestly on us, as though by our own power or holiness we had made this man to walk?" (Acts 3:12 KJV)

He knew his shortcomings.

He also knew his Source!

> "His name, through faith in His name, has made this man strong," (Acts 3:16 NKJV)

That same matchless name has made you strong, man of God!

It is the name of Jesus that gives you the right and the power to operate in the heavenlies. That name, above all others, is the only authority you need to move the needle and level mountains for the Kingdom.

Consider the resounding promises of Scripture.

The following promises are not given to those who think or merely hope that things will change.

They are given to those who boldly pray.

Read slowly, dear friend. These words are written for you...

> "All things, whatsoever ye shall ask in prayer, believing, ye shall receive." (Matthew 21:22)

> "And in that day ye shall ask me nothing. Verily, verily, I say unto you, Whatsoever ye shall ask the Father in my name, he

will give it you. Hitherto have ye asked nothing in my name: ask, and ye shall receive, that your joy may be full." (John 16:23–24)

" "And this is the confidence that we have in him, that, if we ask any thing according to his will, he heareth us: And if we know that he hear us, whatsoever we ask, we know that we have the petitions that we desired of him." (1 John 5:14–15)

" "And I say unto you, Ask, and it shall be given you; seek, and ye shall find; knock, and it shall be opened unto you." (Luke 11:9)

" "If ye then, being evil, know how to give good gifts unto your children: how much more shall your heavenly Father give the Holy Spirit to them that ask him?" (Luke 11:13)

" "Have faith in God. For verily I say unto you, That whosoever shall say unto this mountain, Be thou removed, and be thou cast into the sea; and shall not doubt in his heart, but shall believe that those things which he saith shall come to pass; he shall have whatsoever he saith. Therefore I say unto you, What things soever ye desire, when ye pray, believe that ye receive them, and ye shall have them." (Mark 11:22–24)

"Likewise the Spirit also helpeth our infirmities: for we know not what we should pray for as we ought: but the Spirit itself maketh intercession for us with groanings which cannot be uttered. And he that searcheth the hearts knoweth what is the mind of the Spirit, because he maketh intercession for the saints according to the will of God. And we know that all things work together for good to them that love God, to them who are the called according to his purpose." (Romans 8:26–28)

"Draw near to God, and he will draw near to you." (James 4:8)

"He that spared not his own Son, but delivered him up for us all, how shall he not with him also freely give us all things?" (Romans 8:32)

"Now unto him that is able to do exceeding abundantly above all that we ask or think, according to the power that worketh in us, Unto him be glory in the church by Christ Jesus throughout all ages, world without end. Amen." (Ephesians 3:20–21)

Need we continue? The promises of God to His praying people are more than can be numbered. The name we have been given is above all other names!

CHAPTER 11

GOING DEEP IN PRAYER & WORK

"Men may spurn our appeals, reject our message, oppose our arguments, despise our persons, but they are helpless against our prayers." — J. Sidlow Baxter

THE GREATEST SERVICE you can render mankind is to learn to pray. Prayer gives leverage that goes far beyond natural limits and harnesses the powers of the world to come, unleashing them for an earthly harvest.

Going deep begins with knowing God. Believing and knowing God is the primary work we are called to.

> "This is the work of God, that ye believe on him whom he hath sent." (John 6:29 KJV)

As a believer you have been first called to know God and then work from that place of knowing.

> "And he ordained twelve, that they should be with him, and that he might send them forth..." (Mark 3:14 KJV)

These men were ordained to go, but first, they were called to be.

This lesson from the lives of the early disciples is foundational.

Prosperity begins in the soul. Fruitfulness as men, whether in ministry or business, begins by ensuring that we are vitally united to the Vine.

> "[Live in Me, and I will live in you.] Just as no branch can bear fruit of itself without abiding in (being vitally united to) the vine, neither can you bear fruit unless you abide in Me. I am the Vine; you are the branches. Whoever lives in Me and I in him bears much (abundant) fruit. However, apart from Me [cut off from

vital union with Me] you can do nothing."
(John 15:4–5 AMP)

John the apostle spoke powerfully of this inward connection being the root of outward success.

> "Beloved, I wish above all things that thou mayest prosper and be in health, even as thy soul prospereth." (3 John 1:2 KJV)

In the topsy-turvy culture we inhabit this equation is often inverted. The world wants to convince you that prosperity of pocket will satisfy your soul and bring the happiness you crave. It may for a moment render some relief, but John points out that a clean conscience and a healthy connection to God's purposes, empowered and made possible through a healthy mind and body, will give greater and longer-lasting dividends than any other deal you care to strike.

Another favourite promise box verse, popular on a postcard, is Jeremiah 29:11:

> "For I know the plans I have for you," declares the LORD, "plans to prosper you and not to harm you, plans to give

you   hope   and   a   future."
(Jeremiah 29:11 NIV)

What is often excluded from the conversation is the context of these words.

People love the idea of hope, plans, vibrant destinies, but fail to embrace that the root of the promise is prayer. And by prayer we are not referring to a few incidental requests. Nothing short of deep, repentant, passionate, unreserved seeking of God's face will open the door to this God-filled prosperous future.

> "Then shall ye call upon me, and ye shall go and pray unto me, and I will hearken unto you. And ye shall seek me, and find me, when ye shall search for me with all your heart." (Jeremiah 29:12–13 KJV)

Prayer – the inner work – and **prosperity** – the outer work – are intimately attached.

Jesus warned so clearly of the dangers we will face as we negotiate our pathway through the vanities of the present age.

> "Then the cares and anxieties of the world and distractions of the age, and the

pleasure and delight and false glamour and deceitfulness of riches, and the craving and passionate desire for other things creep in and choke and suffocate the Word, and it becomes fruitless." (Mark 4:19 AMP)

Our challenge in a culture of consumption, with all of the necessities of life clawing for our attention, and a trillion adverts scratching our eyeballs and ears every day, is to keep our craving centred on Christ.

He is the treasure we seek. The field we sell all to own is a field of fruitful favour in His presence and intimate entwinement with His plans. The richest man on earth is the one who has discovered rooted and fruited contentment in the saving grace of God, not the harried hoarder slaving for a bigger barn.

I find myself too often ruffled by the desire for other things, craving significance in all the wrong places. I find the promised pleasures and delights of items that dollars can buy rather too convincing at times.

Satan is a devilish alchemist. He takes the outward tune piped by the world, "I don't have enough", turning it inward to become, "I am not enough."

Tell a lie often enough and big enough and people

will believe it. Politicians through the ages have become amplifiers for satan's schemes in this way for centuries.

The absurdity is that some lies are ones we have wholeheartedly embraced; an entire culture has been swept into the endless chase for significance and happiness based on their accumulation of things.

No time is left for prayer. Work and amassing wealth is the gold-headed, bronze-girdled idol we bow down to today.

What's the lie behind the lure? Can a car really offer significance? Can a can of fizzy drink really deliver bliss? Is our life so shallow that the right logo on our clothing makes us worthy?

Jesus spoke of false glamour and deceitful riches for a reason. Deceit is not deceit if the one who swallows the lie knows what they are guzzling. The very nature of deceit is that we don't realise that we are blind to reality. Consumerism is the western 21st-Century Kool-Aid of choice.

As Leonard Ravenhill scathingly sobbed in his book 'Sodom Had No Bible', *"the mesmerism of materialism has almost completely clogged the channel of blessing."*

This is one of many reasons to place depth of prayer and acquaintance with God as your priority.

Knowing Jesus is ultimately the only thing that really matters.

By nature we pursue things, often with pure intentions, but that intentionality must always be tempered by humble connection to Heaven.

We have responsibilities as men, husbands, and fathers. There is nothing wrong with desire and ambition in this world. The drive to excel in our arena of expertise and calling in the marketplace is a godly one. But treacherous.

If you plan to go deep, go deep in prayer first, and from that place of connection go build, create and sell. Sell as an act of service to others, seeking their best. Make your life count in places more significant than just your bank account.

God's desire is to prosper His people, but not at the cost of integrity.

The rash-like preoccupation with money is a disease we need to inoculate in the secret place of prayer. That way, when cash comes into our hands we will act as stewards not slaves of the riches entrusted to us.

Jesus first, everything else follows.

CHAPTER 12
FEROCIOUS FOCUS - DON'T LET YOUR CLOSET BECOME CROWDED

"Secret praying is the test, the gauge, the conserver of man's relation to God." — E. M. Bounds

WHEN JESUS TAUGHT the hillside crowds about prayer He said:

> "But thou, when thou prayest, enter into thy closet, and when thou hast shut thy door, pray to thy Father which is in secret; and thy Father which seeth in secret shall reward thee openly." (Matthew 6:6 KJV)

Shut the door!

Don't let your closet become crowded.

The closet is a picture of the space you construct

for the presence of God to take priority and precedence in your life.

It is a holy place sanctified and set apart in holy expectation that something special and supernatural will occur.

Satan hates that thought. Your own flesh will fight against being dethroned. Carving out the boundaries of your closet and hammering the pegs into the ground to prepare your spiritual sanctuary takes work and will face resistance within and without.

The ground of your soul that you are possessing for the practice of prayer may have been occupied for many years, overrun by the cares and concerns of this life, the deceitfulness of riches, desire for other things, greedy pursuits, and devilish trespassers.

Brother, it is time to give eviction orders!

The desire for other things must go and the door be firmly slammed in the face of distraction. This does not mean that we neglect our responsibilities. We still build our businesses, bring up our children, love and tend affectionately to our wives. But our totem pole of priority is radically rearranged so the idols of modernity no longer stand at its head.

If the door is not closed to disturbance an entourage of concerns, comparisons, and competitive notions will creep into the closet with you. What is intended to be a holy space becomes crowded with personalities other than the One you are seeking.

Yesterday's concerns will bustle in, seeking to fill the atmosphere with worry. Tomorrow's uncertainties will goad you out of the sanctuary to seek and sort them in your own strength.

If you are not careful, the prayer closet becomes a thoroughfare for any thought that chances by.

This kind of distracted atmosphere is not conductive to effective prayer. The heart and mind bounce here and there, never landing upon any subject long enough to harness it to the will of God and pray it through.

In an age of 3-second attention spans the old school practice of "praying through" is foreign to most men. We want answers and we want them now!

Fervency gives way to urgency and pressing present concerns relegate real Kingdom priorities. In the life of a fierce man or woman of prayer this tendency to dance around must be subdued.

FEROCIOUS FOCUS

Prayer requires your full attention. There is no half-hearted approach to God. He is a consuming fire, and the idea that we can balance worldly ambitions and the wilds of the Spirit is foreign to Scripture.

The first commandment is to love God unreservedly in mind, body, soul, and spirit. There is no room for maybe.

Amusements will seek to barge into your prayer time. Thoughts will push for attention. Niggles will rise to the surface. Negative emotions will elbow their way into your closet attempting to divert your gaze.

Keeping your eyes firmly fixed on Jesus is not easy when your soul has been trained to jump with every ping and vibration.

The life of prayer is not a hurried one. Prayer life is counter-culture. Today's lifestyle of rush, hurry, consumption, accumulation, competition, and comparison conflicts entirely with the pursuit and attainment of the rich, unhurried, and hearty inner life that you crave.

To honestly become a man of the spirit is not something you can conveniently cram into your Day-Timer.

Prayer is life. It demands change and transformation in every area, not just the small space behind the door of your closet for a few minutes of quiet contemplation. Prayer is not a box that you tick.

Fierce focus doesn't happen by accident. Your inputs throughout the day must change, or they will crowd into your closet even when the door has been closed. Priorities and pace must be made subject to the demands of the sanctuary, not the other way around.

Too often prayer is crammed around our day, not our day shaped around prayer.

Prayer is not something you can 'fit in' to your furious over-busy schedule. It will take time, attention, and costly devotion. If you want God's presence and Voice to be more than a side dish, you must sit at the right table.

Jesus is not going to barge into your schedule and force your hand. If your life is crowded with a multitude of minor affairs, He won't push them aside demanding your attention.

Shoo the crowd from your closet and open the door to the King.

> "Behold, I stand at the door, and knock: if any man hear my voice, and open the door, I will come in to him, and will sup with him, and he with me." (Revelation 3:20 KJV)

The door that He's knocking, and wants to step through, is the door you shut to the noise and hurry of the world.

This place of prayer will soon become your most

treasured place on earth because it's here that Heaven breaks in and you get to sup with the Saviour.

May our prayer be the same as that of the God-hungry author and pastor, Andrew Murray:

66 "O, let the place of secret prayer become to me the most beloved spot on earth."

CHAPTER 13
THE BEST WAY TO STAND UP IS ON OUR KNEES

"To get nations back on their feet, we must first get down on our knees." – Billy Graham

DISPUTES, wrangling, and debates resolve diddly squat. Reasonings result in ever more confusion when the arguments believers are hooked into are unreasonable at base. Societies ills and the sexual, social, and the financial confusions that have avalanched over the past decade have no natural solutions because their roots are spiritual.

Spiritual solutions must be employed to overcome spiritual troubles. Darkness is expelled by light, and we desperately need the light of the glorious, power-filled gospel to break through, not with wise and persuasive words, but in demonstration of the Spirit.

> 66 "And my speech and my preaching was not with enticing words of man's wisdom, but in demonstration of the Spirit and of power:" (1 Corinthians 2:4 KJV)

The church has largely resigned their position in the heavenly chairs of authority and decided instead to run programs. Visible, practical social action is essential, but in the absence of spiritual action in the invisible world, the church becomes little more than just another charity.

Our generation now embodies Isaiah's prophetic warning,

> 66 "Woe unto them that call evil good, and good evil; that put darkness for light, and light for darkness; that put bitter for sweet, and sweet for bitter!" (Isaiah 5:20 KJV)

Christianity and virtue are shunned as intolerant. Lifestyles of sin and degradation are flaunted as something to be admired and celebrated. The slave trade is flourishing right under our overfed and cheaply clothed noses. The name of Jesus is blasphemed and silenced, whist false gods are pacified and pandered to with politically correct (yet wholly incorrect) concessions.

Dear brothers, the arena we fight in is not a natural one. Debate, strife, and dispute are not sharp enough weapons to fight these ideological battles.

The only way to truly stand up is on our knees!

Like the mighty Acts of old, when faced with intimidation and society's wrath, the recourse of the saints was not to swot up on the most eloquent way to pacify their detractors.

They knew then as we must now that there is no natural answer to supernatural opposition.

You don't find the early church fawning to the demands of their cultural puppet-masters. Earthly governments, while respected, were never exalted above the heavenly authority and commission of Christ. They did, however, recognise that heavenly directives cannot be obeyed without heaven's empowerment.

> "They lifted up their voice to God with one accord, and said, Lord, thou *art* God, which hast made heaven, and earth, and the sea, and all that in them is: Who by the mouth of thy servant David hast said,

Why did the heathen rage, and the people imagine vain things? … Lord, behold their threatenings: and grant unto thy servants, that with all boldness they may speak thy word, By stretching forth thine hand to heal; and that signs and wonders may be done by the name of thy holy child Jesus." (Acts 4:24–31 KJV)

They felt their naked need to be clothed with demonstration of the power that they preached. Words alone are simply not enough to cut through the noise. We need the Holy Ghost, brother! The church without the Holy Ghost is like a vehicle without an engine, fuel, or steering. It's an empty shell, spouting an empty message, banging a tinny, repulsive religious gong.

Paul described it as *"Having a form of godliness, but denying the power thereof." (2 Timothy 3:5 KJV)*

In response to the believers prayer we read from Acts chapter 4, something remarkable happened.

> "When they had prayed, the place was shaken where they were assembled together; and they were all filled with the Holy Ghost, and they spake the word of God with boldness." (Acts 4:31 KJV)

Such is our need today. A mighty shaking, a glorious infilling, and a boldness born from encounter not empty eloquence.

Let me highlight these four words for you:

"When they had prayed."

Our nations need a move of God. We have strayed far beyond the line of no return, and without an earth shaking significant awakening, the church becomes more irrelevant by the second.

When the people of God are almost indistinguishable from the culture they are steeped into how can we ever proclaim a transformative pathway to new life?

Prayer and prayer alone is sufficient to change society, because when the church hits its knees it changes us. Repentance, a holy turnaround and transformation, begins first in the house of God.

Without a thorough examination of our lives, a deep repentant return to the Bible, and a fervent fire-filled dedication to the closet of prayer, the tides that threaten to drown the voice of God's people in darkness will continue to rise.

Men of God are needed. Ferocious men of prayer!

God's means have not changed. He is the Master of time, not dutifully moving with the trends and forced to adapt his methods to be more acceptable to the materialistic masses.

The foolish notion that unusual supernatural manifestations of God's presence and power will repel the world indicate just how far we have fallen from the Biblical norm.

The world is waiting for God to turn up!

The fact that He is so starkly absent from the majority of church services and the lives of those who claim to follow Him is the only thing repulsive to a watching world.

Come, Holy Spirit, turn over the tables, and let your house become again a holy house of prayer.

CHAPTER 14
RENDING HEAVENS BEGINS WITH RENDING HEARTS

"The coming revival must begin with a great revival of prayer. It is in the closet, with the door shut, that the sound of abundance of rain will first be heard. An increase of secret prayer with ministers will be the sure harbinger of blessing." — Andrew Murray

THE MIGHTY WORK of revival is often pictured in the Scriptures as rain.

Rain that comes when hearts return.

66 "Come, and let us return unto the LORD: for he hath torn, and he will heal us; he hath smitten, and he will bind us up. After two days will he revive us: in the

third day he will raise us up, and we shall live in his sight. Then shall we know, if we follow on to know the LORD: his going forth is prepared as the morning; and he shall come unto us as the rain, as the latter and former rain unto the earth." (Hosea 6:1–3 KJV)

If the revival work of God is rain, we need a flood!

Prayer and revival are so entwined throughout history that no honest student could ever say a mighty work of God is possible without there first being a mighty work of prayer.

The famous British reformer, John Wesley, is quoted as saying, *"God does nothing except in response to believing prayer."*

And you, man of God, are sanctioned to offer supplications for a revival work among the nations. You are commended to ask:

66   "Ask ye of the LORD rain in the time of the latter rain; so the LORD shall make bright clouds, and give them showers of rain, to every one grass in the field." (Zechariah 10:1 KJV)

This holy consecration begins with hearts that are hungry and thirsty for God Himself.

The hard and calloused state of our hearts and consciences will be softened by the early rains. I well remember the magnificent outpourings of joy in the early 1990's. Our fallow empty fields were broken up by early rains of delight in God.

> "Sow to yourselves in righteousness, reap in mercy; break up your fallow ground: for it is time to seek the LORD, till he come and rain righteousness upon you." (Hosea 10:12 KJV)

There are also heavier rains that drive deeper into the heart, no less joyful in their fruits, but painful in what they expose. Grudges are washed away in the deluge, as are ego and self-centred empire building. Unforgiveness and greed are purged, forced into the gulleys and driven out to sea.

Such works of grace are to be treasured, for it is the goodness of God that leads us to deep repentance and renewed faith.

It has been said that God loves us as we are, but loves us too much to allow us to stay that way.

If you hope for more than just a religious makeover, God will go deep indeed. The work of prayer to which we are called is a heart labor and excavation of the soul, the breaking up of the hardened uncultivated ground, and the 'turning' can be terrible.

Evan Roberts, the firebrand of revivalist knew what it is to be turned.

In 1903, Evan was just 25 years old. Roberts found himself at an evangelistic event where a man named Seth Joshua was preaching and heard the preacher pray, "Lord, bend us!"

This became Evan's battlecry.

Of the experience he wrote:

"I felt a living power pervading my bosom. It took my breath away and my legs trembled exceedingly. This living power became stronger and stronger as each one prayed, until I felt it would tear me apart. My whole bosom was a turmoil and if I had not prayed it would have burst ... I fell on my knees with my arms over the seat in front of me. My face was bathed in perspiration, and the tears flowed in streams. I cried out, 'Bend me, bend me!!' It was God's commending love which bent me ... I was filled with compassion for those who must bend at the judgement, and I wept. Following that, the salvation of the human soul was solemnly impressed on me. I felt ablaze with the desire to go through the length and breadth of Wales to tell of the Saviour."

The unquenchable fire that gripped Evan's soul woke him for weeks at one in the morning to pray for hours. Intense love of God and a deep desire to see others come to Christ purged his soul of every other pursuit. He began to pray together with a few others: "Bend us, Lord."

Within nine months, over 100,000 people had come to Christ.

Perhaps the reason we have not seen magnificent t outpourings marked by startling salvation in our generation is the heart-rending price that must first be paid.

In his book, *Revival Praying*, Leonard Ravenhill expounds on the price and promise found in Psalm 126:6:

> "He that goeth forth and weepeth, bearing precious seed, shall doubtless come again with rejoicing, bringing his sheaves with him."

He speaks of the lonely work of spiritual sowing in prayer.

"The price tag for effective prayer differs for every one of us, but the fact remains that a true Spirit-praying person will have much of his domestic life shattered. On the human level, we each tread our path to the skies alone ... Alone he goeth weeping, bearing seed. There are no mass production lines in grace ... Today when rough land is being broken up, a farmer often drives his horses or tractor alone. The weather is inclement, the pace slow, the going difficult, but visualizing the harvest time, he holds on – alone. Yet when that time comes, he calls in many to gather in the precious grain. Thus it is in the spiritual world: few break up the fallow ground in hearts and sow it with precious seed, but an army may be needed to gather the God-blessed results."

Such can be the work of God through a broken heart.

Rending of the heart precedes the rending of the heavens!

> "And rend your heart ... and turn unto the LORD your God: for he is gracious and merciful, slow to anger, and of great kindness, and repenteth him of the evil."
> (Joel 2:13 KJV)

The impassioned prayer of a rent heart calls for

more than mediocrity. Nothing but the manifest presence and power of the Almighty will suffice.

> "Oh that thou wouldest rend the heavens, that thou wouldest come down, that the mountains might flow down at thy presence, As *when* the melting fire burneth, the fire causeth the waters to boil, to make thy name known to thine adversaries, *that* the nations may tremble at thy presence!" (Isaiah 64:1–2 KJV)

THE FOUNTAINS OF THE DEEP

A worldwide flood of God's saving grace is needed. No program of ministry can provide that. Only prayer. Deep travailing prayer capable of opening an ocean of mercy into which millions of souls will be swept.

Noah's flood is described so eloquently in Genesis 7:11:

> "…all the fountains of the great deep were broken up, and the windows of heaven were opened."

The great deeps of our hearts must be broken up

to meet the deluge that Papa wants to send from Heaven.

Pitiful, polite, costless petitions centred on our own needs are shamefully inadequate for the hour. Deep, wordless groans are called for. Strong crying and tears like our Saviour's.

> "Who in the days of his flesh, when he had offered up prayers and supplications with strong crying and tears unto him that was able to save him from death, and was heard in that he feared" (Hebrews 5:7 KJV)

How can a broken world be reached by an unbroken church? How can a world steeped in pride be convicted by a church so self-absorbed?

I speak as one wholly guilty of all that I shine the light upon. When the prophet's fingers points, his accusation toward me would be, *"You are that man!"* *(2 Samuel 12:7).*

For all my indignation, I find myself in need of bending.

"Bend me, Lord."

CHAPTER 15
STIR YOURSELF

"History is silent about revivals that did not begin with prayer." — Edwin Orr

MANY WAIT for God to make the first move. If He wants me to pray He'll make me do it they reason. And God indeed is the Source of all impassioned prayer, but not apart from a hungry heart.

We see a pattern throughout Scripture with regard to prayer.

"Seek first *and* all these things will be added.

"Pray in secret *and* thy Father who sees will reward thee openly."

"Draw near to God *and* He will draw near to you."

"Ask *and* it will be given."

"Seek *and* ye will find."

"Knock *and* it will be opened to you."

You seek. You pray. You draw near.

And when you do … God!

Isaiah lamented,

> "There is none that calleth upon thy name, that stirreth up himself to take hold of thee." (Isaiah 64:7 KJV)

Man of God, stir thyself!

Stop waiting for God to do the stirring.

Position yourself to be stirred, brother, by sheer act of will if necessary.

Not flesh and fury, but humble acceptance of the call. Make concrete changes to your lifestyle and your use of time that clearly indicate to the Holy Ghost that you mean business.

Step into the closet and shut the door!

In my early days of learning to pray that was about the sum total of my knowhow. I knew how to step into a bare room, and close the door. I turned the key in the lock, and told myself, "You are here, David, for the next two hours. So you may as well learn to pray!"

Stood in that room, clueless as to what to say and

how to even begin, my odyssey into the Father's grace began.

My first prayers for several such sessions can be summed up in the following way.

"Ok, God, here I am. I have no idea how to pray, hear your voice, or even where to begin. But I'm here, and the door is closed. If you don't teach me, we're both going to be very bored. I'm stirring myself to take hold of you, but I need You to take hold of me and show me the way. Here I am, Lord."

Those sessions became morning, noon, and night.

I read somewhere in Psalms that David shaped his day around prayer.

66 "As for me, I will call upon God; and the LORD shall save me. Evening, and morning, and at noon, will I pray, and cry aloud: and he shall hear my voice." (Psalm 55:16–17 KJV)

An hour praying in tongues before work. An hour on my knees, crouched in my car with my head buried in the passenger seat during my lunch hour, and an hour to crown the day before sleep.

This was my bootcamp. My place of learning.

Did it happen in an instant?

Did God break in only when it was convenient for me and my busy schedule?

Was I wrong to dedicate my lunch break to tongue talking? Dumb to rise at 4am to seek the King? Over zealous to end my day with praise?

You want to know why I pursued in this manner? Not because I was strong or holy. Far from it. Quite the opposite in fact.

I was weak and I knew it.

I was scared and didn't know how not to be.

Jesus saved me from dark despair and placed me in His Kingdom. Utter bewilderment at the goodness of God gripped my curiosity. If He could be so incredible to me as a sinner and meet me while I was actively pursuing things He calls abominable, what in the world would He do if I came to Him as a friend?

Every ounce of my being wanted to know Him more fully.

Maybe you share that passion?

Prayer is the avenue that God has given to us for that very purpose. Fellowship and participation with God begins in prayer.

Why prayer? I can only conjecture, but I believe the following may have some bearing.

Because the flesh sizzles in the secret place.

Ego is fried when no-one else is listening.

Haste and hurry are unwelcome and counterproductive in the King's presence, so our self-reliant busyness is laid bare.

The place of prayer is where the old man goes to die, and the new man is discovered.

All that the flesh loves the Spirit loathes. Both cannot sit comfortably in the same room.

> "The carnal mind is enmity against God: for it is not subject to the law of God, neither indeed can be. So then they that are in the flesh cannot please God. But ye are not in the flesh, but in the Spirit, if so be that the Spirit of God dwell in you." (Romans 8:7–9 KJV)

In the place of prayer, hours not minutes, the grip of the flesh weakens, and Spirt takes hold. You will become aware of who you really are in Christ. Not just by assent to the words on the pages of the Bible, but through vital experience of the living Word at work in your life.

It begins when we call on His name, stirring ourselves to take hold of God.

CHAPTER 16
TRAVAIL TO PREVAIL

"The prayer that prevails is not the work of lips and fingertips. It is the cry of a broken heart and the travail of a stricken soul." — Samuel Chadwick

TRAVAILING in prayer is a concept largely alien to modern Western churches.

> **"My little children, of whom I travail in birth again until Christ be formed in you"** (Galatians 4:19 KJV)

Paul spoke of his work of prayer as travail. We partner with the Holy Spirit who acts as midwife to birth the purposes of God through us as we pray. It's not always pretty or eloquent. Expect hot emotions and many tears. Words fall away and groanings ensue when the aching heart of God breaks into the prayer room.

Spurgeon writes of this manner of prayer when he said, *"Groanings which cannot be uttered are often prayers which cannot be refused. "*

This kind of manifestation is common to every revival and awakening we have witnessed throughout the centuries, but starkly absent in many modern churches.

Scripture speaks of God shouting aloud as warrior against His enemies, and crying, gasping, and panting like a travailing woman.

> "Jehovah will go forth as a mighty man; he will stir up *his* zeal like a man of war: he will cry, yea, he will shout aloud; he will do mightily against his enemies. I have long time holden my peace; I have been still, and refrained myself: *now* will I cry out like a travailing woman; I will gasp and pant together." (Isaiah 42:13–14 ASV)

Travail in prayer is not something we enter into by an act of will or want, it is a leading deep by the

Holy Ghost to feel and express but for a moment the depth of His compassions for broken humanity.

I have myself entered into this kind of soul-gripping intercession on a number of occasions and felt the consuming passion of God at work in a powerful way. The experience is one of intensity, and at the same time abandon and yielding, rolled into one. The praying man will feel the unction take hold and strong crying erupt from the inner well, but the expression of that inner cry is one that flows from disengagement of self and yielding to God's presence at work in and through. Groaning and travail occur when the heart gate opens wide so the heavy prayer waters can flow unencumbered.

The Diaries of David Brainerd, made famous when Revivalist Jonathan Edwards published them, speak much of this heart rending form of prayer.

The Scriptures declare:

> "As soon as Zion travailed, she brought forth her children." (Isaiah 66:8 ASV)

Brainerd's overwhelming desire to see souls in the grip of satan saved and swept into the Kingdom embody this kind of impolite praying.

He speaks in his diaries of whole nights and days

gripped with intense desire for the souls of the people he was called to serve.

Just a handful of quotes from its pages shine a light on why he experienced one of the most remarkable revivals ever recorded.

"This morning about nine I withdrew to the woods for prayer. I was in such anguish that when I rose from my knees I felt extremely weak and overcome, and the sweat ran down my face and body ... I cared not where or how I lived, or what hardships I went through, so that I could but gain souls for Christ. I continued in this frame all the evening and night."

"I set apart this day for secret fasting and prayer. Just at night the Lord visited me marvelously. I wrestled for an ingathering of souls ... I was in such an agony from sun half an hour, till near dark, that I was all over wet with sweat. Oh, my dear Saviour did sweat blood for poor souls. I went to bed with my heart wholly set on God."

Such prayer is not something we can conjure up, but it is something we can open up to. Nay, something we can welcome!

Slay the desire for seeker friendly atmospheres where the Holy Ghost is gagged. Some services may be shaped for such, but the prayer meeting should be fire friendly!

When believers gather to pray the atmosphere should be combustible, filled with the fiery incense of worship, and our intercession should be incendiary.

The prayer meeting is the birthing house of the church, with many a man throwing his head between his knees, face to the floor, lifting cries to the throne that God's will be done on earth as in Heaven.

When the time has come for the waters to break, nothing can hold them back.

66 "Elijah went up to the top of Carmel; and he cast himself down upon the earth, and put his face between his knees." (1 Kings 18:42 KJV)

This intercessory picture shows Elijah taking the position most commonly used by labouring ladies of his day.

Seven times the contractions that birthed an

outpouring on Israel gripped him, until a cloud appeared signifying what was to come.

Elijah's manner of prayer is picked up by James who says:

66 "The effective, fervent prayer of a righteous man avails much. Elijah was a man with a nature like ours, and he prayed earnestly that it would not rain; and it did not rain on the land for three years and six months. And he prayed again, and the heaven gave rain, and the earth produced its fruit." (James 5:16–18 NKJV)

Surely we too want to be effective. We need to see the glory and presence of God restored to the house.

I have quoted Leonard Ravenhill several times in this book, and the following statement seemed so apt I could not leave it out:

66 "At God's counter there are no 'SALE DAYS,' for the price of revival is ever the same - TRAVAIL."

In prayer you get what you pay for. Deal in small

change, the leftover drops of the day's affairs, and you'll experience leftover results.

Fervency is required, and requires much of the praying man.

Fervency in prayer is the firepower that breaks down resistance.

> "Earnest (heartfelt, continued) prayer … makes tremendous power available [dynamic in its working]." (James 5:16 AMP)

William Booth, the founder of the Salvation Army and a force for God in his generation said of prayer:

> "You must pray with all your might. That does not mean saying your prayers, or sitting gazing about in church or chapel with eyes wide open while someone else says them for you. It means fervent, effectual, untiring wrestling with God."

He also warned,

> "This kind of prayer be sure the devil and the world and your own indolent,

unbelieving nature will oppose. They will pour water on this flame."

Dare I say, many a church may oppose it too. The call to prayer is not one to popularity or political correctness. Most often it is not public. The praying men and women I have had the privilege to know all craved the privacy and solitude that allows them freedom to flow with the mighty rivers of God from their hearts.

Travail is messy, unsettling, not in the slightest bit flesh-friendly. Passionate, prevailing prayer, demands that we lay aside our desire to look good and be right. It is visceral, violent, passionate, fierce, and fixed on seeing the purpose of God fulfilled with no return.

Much like a woman in labour, once the pangs kick in, and assuming the pray-er continues to yield and doesn't not allow fear or reason to rob him of the moment, the contractions will continue until peace floods his soul.

In my experience travail can continue for some time, but when the purpose is accomplished (you will feel a shift take place in the spirit) peace and joy follow.

Jesus described the process thus:

66 "A woman when she is in travail hath sorrow, because her hour is come: but as soon as she is delivered of the child, she remembereth no more the anguish, for joy that a man is born into the world." (John 16:21 KJV)

There is victory in Jesus. He leads us in triumph.

This powerful expression of God's Spirit interceding through His people is a sure path to taste true victory and overcome the powers of darkness!

CHAPTER 17
WORSHIP IS OUR WEAPON

THE PEOPLE of God do not fight with guns and sticks. Such are the weapons of man-made religion.

Our weapon is worship.

Worship breaks chains. Worship routs enemy armies, throwing confusion in their ranks.

Worship tumbles stubborn walls, and brings down the holy fire of Heaven.

The manifestations of worship and warfare we read throughout the Scriptures are equally manifest in the invisible battles that we fight today; binding and loosing, breaking bondages, confusing the enemy and causing him to flee.

Worship is not the five song sandwich at the head of a service, the starter dish for the sermon, or the parting sing-song before Sunday lunch.

Worship is a weapon!

Formidable spiritual firepower is unleashed from fiery hearts in the form of worship and sets Heaven's hosts in motion. Angelic armies are activated in radical array against mankind's real enemies, the invisible puppeteers in the spiritual realm.

As A.W.Tozer so rightly taught, the armies of God on earth are brought into one accord through worship, not by efforts to accommodate or foster a false unity based on fickle feelings:

> "Has it ever occurred to you that one hundred pianos all tuned to the same fork are automatically tuned to each other? They are of one accord by being tuned, not to each other, but to another standard to which each one must individually bow. So one hundred worshipers meeting together, each one looking away to Christ, are in heart nearer to each other than they could possibly be, were they to become 'unity' conscious and turn their eyes away from God to strive for closer fellowship."

It is in honest worship that we take our place in line, and become and accomplish more than we could alone. Even privately ensconced in our secret closet, worship connects you to this universal campaign.

The battle we fight is not a natural one so our weapons must therefore be spiritual.

> "For we wrestle not against flesh and blood, but against principalities, against powers, against the rulers of the darkness of this world, against spiritual wickedness in high places." (Ephesians 6:12 KJV)

> "(For the weapons of our warfare are not carnal, but mighty through God to the pulling down of strong holds;)" (2 Corinthians 10:4 KJV)

The sword we carry is in our mouths, the two-edged sword of Word and worship, exalting the King.

> "Let the high praises of God be in their mouth, and a twoedged sword in their hand; To execute vengeance upon the heathen, and punishments upon the people; To bind their kings with chains, and their nobles with fetters of iron; To execute upon them the judgment written:

this honour have all his saints. Praise ye the LORD." (Psalm 149:6–9 KJV)

There is good reason that the worshippers were sent at the head of the armies. The Lord fights on behalf of those who worship Him. We can employ the same military tactic today, lifting the strong arm of praise before petition.

> "… he appointed singers unto the LORD, and that should praise the beauty of holiness, as they went out before the army, and to say, Praise the LORD; for his mercy endureth for ever. And when they began to sing and to praise, the LORD set ambushments against the children of Ammon, Moab, and mount Seir, which were come against Judah; and they were smitten." (2 Chronicles 20:21–22 KJV)

I urge you to go to the armoury, the Word of God, and stock your vocabulary to wage a skilful warfare. The Scriptures are replete with words that can be employed in the heat of battle.

When discouragement steps onto the field, brandishing his lies, there's a Word of courage to cut him down.

When fear flies, showering reasons to turn back and run, deposited Scriptures will rise from your heart to rout his attack.

Spirit and truth work together, and the Father seeks such to worship Him. Men who know Truth and are prepared to pull proclamations from their quiver when the heat is high will taste victory.

Like the golden thread woven throughout all of prayer, worship wins when all else seems lost. Worship is a natural response to God's good graces and the weapon of choice when God seems distant.

Worship the King, dear brother. Lift your voice in praise to the One in whom is no shadow of turning. Praise Him for the answers you expect and victories you will win. Praise Him for His mercies, and for His marvels. Miracles happen in an atmosphere where the Miracle worker is enthroned.

> "Thou art holy, O thou that inhabitest the praises of Israel. Our fathers trusted in thee: they trusted, and thou didst deliver them. They cried unto thee, and were delivered: they trusted in thee, and were not confounded." (Psalm 22:3–5 KJV)

I will employ the words of my brother, A.W. Tozer, one more time to spur your heart to high thoughts:

"The Church has surrendered her once lofty concept of God and has substituted for it one so low, so ignoble, as to be utterly unworthy of thinking, worshiping men. This she has not done deliberately, but little by little and without her knowledge; and her very unawareness only makes her situation all the more tragic ...

Millions call themselves by His name, it is true, and pay some token homage to Him, but a simple test will show how little He is really honored among them. Let the average man be put to the proof on the question of who or what is ABOVE, and his true position will be exposed. Let him be forced into making a choice between God and money, between God and men, between God and personal ambition, God and self, God and human love, and God will take second place every time. Those other things will be exalted above. However the man may protest, the proof is in the choice he makes day after day throughout his life ...

We must never rest until everything inside us worships God."

God is truly worthy of praise. Worship is the air of Heaven, the oxygen of the born-again pilgrim living in the airless atmosphere of a fallen world.

Lift your voice in worship and wage warfare with all that stands between you and the victories God has set you apart to win.

CHAPTER 18
A TENDER HEART IS TINDER FOR THE SPARKS OF REVIVAL

> *"God, make me a man with thick skin and a*
> *soft heart. Make me a man who is tough*
> *and tender. Make me tough so I can*
> *handle life. Make me tender so I can*
> *love people. God, make me a man." –*
> *Darrin Patrick*

A TENDER, receptive spirit will always be pulled to the practice of prayer. Love for God is evidenced in longing for His presence, fascination with His perfections, and a desire to plumb His depths.

Prayer is the only avenue to experience the great mercies of God in manifestation.

It begins first with the heart, hungry for heaven.

This is the inception of a strong and powerful

prayer life. Hunger for God, and desire to know Jesus through His Spirit.

Don't seek to be a great man of prayer, desire instead to be a man of great love for Christ. It is He who draws us to Himself when the heart refuses to be satisfied with the world's trinkets.

Jonathan Edwards wrote:

> "O! One hour with God infinitely exceeds all the pleasures and delights of this lower world."

Ravenhill observed:

> "A man who is intimate with God is not intimidated by man."

How beautiful the out-breathing of Andrew Murray's heart when he said:

> "O, let the place of secret prayer become to me the most beloved spot on earth."

For all the fury of the pages I have written here, the chief aim is to provoke my brothers to the one essential work.

> "Then said they unto him, What shall we do, that we might work the works of God? Jesus answered and said unto them, This is the work of God, that ye believe on him whom he hath sent." (John 6:28–29 KJV)

The work of God is not preaching, not even prayer. The true work of a man's heart and his true purpose in life is to believe on the One whom the Father sent.

Outside this relationship with Christ all the energies of man, even wrapped in religious garb, are powerless to accomplish their desired end.

To see the mighty hand of God moving in our day, and to work the works He has prepared for you, the prime directive is to know Him.

Eternal results flow when we connect with eternity.

> "And this is life eternal, that they might know thee the only true God, and Jesus Christ, whom thou hast sent." (John 17:3 KJV)

Scripture teaches, indeed invites us to intimacy, with the words:

> "He has made everything beautiful in its time. He also has planted eternity in men's hearts *and* minds [a divinely implanted sense of a purpose working through the ages which nothing under the sun but God alone can satisfy], yet so that men cannot find out what God has done from the beginning to the end." (Ecclesiastes 3:11 AMP)

Nothing else will ever satisfy you, brother.

There's a divine implanted hunger in your heart that nothing under the sun will ever satisfy. A purpose bigger than yourself, rooted in relationship with your God.

It is a high calling to secret seeking. In the place of intimacy your Father wants to reveal Truth to your heart that will unshackle you from the beggarly offerings this lower world bids for your time and attention.

His call to the closet of prayer is tender, and in the place of prayer your heart will hear kindness unheard of on this earth.

> "There I will meet with you and, from above the mercy seat, from between the two cherubim that are upon the ark of the

Testimony, I will speak intimately with you of all which I will give you in commandment to the Israelites." (Exodus 25:22 AMPLIFIED)

When confronted with the love of God John Wesley recalled that "the things of earth grew strangely dim." The brightness of this world's greatest glory is trifling compared to knowing Jesus.

He is known in the place of prayer.

Here in the sanctuary we are stripped of all that hides our hearts, and we are fully known. Your manly frame may bristle when confronted by such affection, but the undoing of your bravado will reveal something far more beautiful.

You, my brother, are a man of prayer.

Known of God.

Making God known.

A ferocious and fearless lover of Christ.

This is your calling and your eternal purpose on earth.

History is being written on scrolls yet to be unfurled, and your work of grace in the secret place will mark your name for eternity in the roll of honour on that great day of reckoning.

CHAPTER 19
PLAYGROUND OR BATTLEGROUND

"God shapes the world by prayer. The more
praying there is in the world the better
the world will be, the mightier the forces
against evil." — E.M. Bounds

IN THE SERIOUSNESS of our subject, and the tearing of the heart revival preaching stirs, I cannot leave the picture incomplete without pointing one more time to Jesus.

His wisdom is many faceted. His ways beyond our own.

In the breaking there is healing. In the emptying a fullness beyond compare.

God is a consuming fire, yet a Father of infinite compassions and mercy.

We are indeed on a battleground, and the warrior

call is one to a straitened life, but it is nevertheless a life of joy unspeakable where spiritual discipline delivers delights of spirit and soul unmatched in the kingdoms of the world.

The life of prayer is not a heavy yoke to bear. It is the joyful privilege of God's lovers to share His heart.

The invitation to intensity is also the call to intimacy.

God has secrets He shares with only some. There are places in His pavilion reserved for His lovers that mere acquaintances will never visit.

> "The secret of the LORD is with them that fear him; and he will shew them his covenant." (Psalm 25:14 KJV)

Will you splash on the surface, or dive to the deeps?

Do you dare allow the affections of your God to fill your heart?

Will He find in you a man after His heart, ready to give voice to His deepest yearnings?

Can the Holy Ghost trust you with His requests, and lift them up through you?

A man of shallows only makes requests of God, but the man of covenant has entered a holy partnership where God makes requests of him.

As with Abraham God will ask, "How can I do this thing without first speaking to my friend." (Genesis 18:17). The call to intercession is born of holy friendship.

Oh, for such intimate communion today. To be one upon whom our Saviour can call.

Our Father is not removed from His creation. His eyes see all; the four-year old baby girl almost split by the perversions of paedophiles sacrificing innocents to the lustful spirit that has possessed them; the drug addict shooting poison in their arm, robbed of dignity, and dead before their death; the helpless mother unable to feed her starving swollen-bellied children while the other half satiate their greed with extravagant displays of selfish indulgence.

Need we continue?

God is an emotional being. His feelings run deeper and are more intense than any human heart could stand. He weeps. He laughs. He yearns. He rejoices.

The life of prayer is not a sterile list that we dutifully tick each day, it's a call to know the goodness and severity of the Saviour. To share His matchless joy, and be broken by His all-knowing sorrow.

This, my dear friend, is a manly call.

A call to know your God, and do exploits.

> "the people that do know their God shall be strong, and do exploits." (Daniel 11:32 KJV)

I so want to tell you it is easy. That there's an effortless, painless path to knowing the heart of God. That you can play your way to resurrection life. But I cannot.

If you heed this call and close the closet door, you will surely know delights that others only dream of, but your heart will also break with the affections of your Saviour for the souls outside that door.

Our beautiful Jesus does not need lukewarm men. Hot or cold is His call. Nothing in between.

My urgent plea is that you would be aflame with fresh resolve to serve your Saviour in the secret place of fierce prayer!

CHAPTER 20
PRACTICAL INSTRUCTION IN PRAYER

"All you need to do to learn to pray is to pray." — Wesley L Duewel

THERE IS a reason this chapter is short.

Wesley Duewel already offered the best lesson on prayer you'll ever learn. In just twelve words he sums up all the libraries of prayerful instruction the world has amassed.

> **"All you need to do to learn to pray is to pray."**

More are the delights behind the door than all the world will ever offer.

The greatest need of our day is men who will step into the closet and seek God above all else.

When you do, your personal prayer Coach, and the One who will infuse your prayers with other-worldly efficacy, will lead and teach you.

The Holy Ghost awaits.

> "But the anointing which ye have received of him abideth in you, and ye need not that any man teach you: but as the same anointing teacheth you of all things, and is truth, and is no lie, and even as it hath taught you, ye shall abide in him." (1 John 2:27 KJV)

The sweetest and most beautiful hours on earth are spent in fellowship with Him.

Like a fish for water. A bird for air. Man is made for God's presence.

The anointing will lead you to a place of holy abiding. The sheer delights reserved for you in the secret place are beyond any description.

My prayer is that this book will cause you to turn the key in the closet door with fresh expectation, and seek the Living God with passionate resolve.

Man of God, this is indeed your true and most richly rewarded calling in life.

Pray!

CHAPTER 21
KINDLING QUOTES

66 "The most critical need of the church at this moment is men, bold men, free men. The church must seek, in prayer and much humility, the coming again of men made of the stuff of which prophets and martyrs are made." — Aiden Wilson Tozer

66 "Could not but think, as I have often remarked to others, that much more of true religion consists in deep humility, brokenness of heart, and an abasing sense of barrenness and want of grace and holiness than most who are called Christians imagine" — David Brainerd

"I consider that the chief dangers which confront the coming century will be religion without the Holy Ghost, Christianity without Christ, forgiveness without repentance, salvation without regeneration, politics without God, and heaven without hell." — William Booth

"The greatness of a man's power is the measure of his surrender." — William Booth

"Put your ear down to the Bible, and hear Him bid you go and pull sinners out of the fire of sin. Put your ear down to the burdened, agonized heart of humanity, and listen to its pitiful wail for help." — William Booth

"THE GREAT NEED of our world, our nation, and our churches is people who know how to prevail in prayer. Moments of pious wishes blandly expressed to God once or twice a day will bring little change on earth or among the people. Kind thoughts expressed to Him in five or six sentences, after reading a paragraph or two of mildly religious sentiments once a day from some devotional writing, will not bring the kingdom of God to earth or shake the gates of hell and repel the attacks of evil on our culture and our civilization." — Wesley L. Duewel

"Prevailing prayer is prayer that pushes right through all difficulties and obstacles, drives back all the opposing forces of Satan, and secures the will of God. Its purpose is to accomplish God's will on earth. Prevailing prayer is prayer that not only takes the initiative but continues on the offensive for God until spiritual victory is won." — Wesley L Duewel

"I had been heaping up my devotions before God, fasting, praying, and pretending, and indeed really thinking sometimes, that I was aiming at the glory of God; whereas I never once truly intended it, but only my own happiness." — David Brainerd

"A man may study because his brain is hungry for knowledge, even Bible knowledge. But he prays because his soul is hungry for God." — Leonard Ravenhill

❝ "Abiding fully means praying much." — Andy Murray

❝ "How can you pull down strongholds of Satan if you don't even have the strength to turn off your TV?" — Leonard Ravenhill

❝ "But you know if God should stamp eternity or even judgment on our eyeballs, or if you'd like on the fleshy table of our hearts I am quite convinced we'd be a very, very different tribe of people, God's people, in the world today. We live too much in time, we're too earth bound. We see as other men see, we think as other men think. We invest our time as the world invests it. We're supposed to be a different breed of people. I believe that the church of Jesus Christ needs a new revelation of the majesty of God. We're all going to stand one day, can you imagine it- at the judgment seat of Christ to give an account for the deeds done in the body.

This is the King of kings, and He's the Judge of judges, and it's the Tribunal of tribunals, and there's no court of appeal after it. The verdict is final." — Leonard Ravenhill

"Do not have as your motive the desire to be known as a praying man. Get an inner chamber in which to pray where no one knows you are praying, shut the door, and talk to God in secret." — Oswald Chambers

"The man who mobilizes the Christian church to pray will make the greatest contribution to world evangelization in history." — Andrew Murray

"Persistent calling upon the name of the Lord breaks through every stronghold of the devil, for nothing is impossible with God. For Christians in these troubled times there is simply no other way." — Jim Cymbala

"Does the Bible ever say anywhere from Genesis to Revelation, 'My house shall be

called a house of preaching'? Does it ever say, 'My house shall be called a house of music'? Of course not. The Bible does say, 'My house shall be called a house of prayer for all nations'. Preaching, music, the reading of the Word - these things are fine; I believe in and practice all of them. But they must never override prayer as the defining mark of God's dwelling. the honest truth is that I have seen God do more in people's lives during ten minutes of real prayer than in ten of my sermons."
— Jim Cymbala

"Your future and mine are determined by this one thing: seeking after the Lord."
— Jim Cymbala

"If revival is being withheld from us it is because some idol remains still enthroned; because we still insist in placing our reliance in human schemes; because we still refuse to face the unchangeable truth that it is not by might, but by My Spirit."
— Jonathan Goforth

"In the Irish Revival of 1859, people became so weak that they could not get back to their homes. Men and women would fall by the wayside and would be found hours later pleading with God to save their souls. They felt that they were slipping into hell and that nothing else in life mattered but to get right with God... To them eternity meant everything. Nothing else was of any consequence. They felt that if God did not have mercy on them and save them, they were doomed for all time to come." — Oswald J. Smith

"Prayer meetings are dead affairs when they are merely asking sessions; there is adventure, hope and life when they are believing sessions, and the faith is corporately, practically and deliberately affirmed." — Norman Grubb

"Oh, how few find time for prayer! There is time for everything else, time to sleep and time to eat, time to read the newspaper and the novel, time to visit friends, time for everything else under the sun, but-no time for prayer, the most important of all things, the one great essential!" — Oswald J. Smith

"I am perfectly confident that the man who does not spend hours alone with God will never know the anointing of the Holy Spirit. The world must be left outside until God alone fills the vision...God has promised to answer prayer. It is not that He is unwilling, for the fact is, He is more willing to give than we are to receive. But the trouble is, we are not ready…" — Oswald J. Smith

"Revival, as contrasted with a Holy Ghost atmosphere is a clean-cut breakthrough of the Spirit, a sweep of Holy Ghost power, bending the hearts of hardened sinners as the wheat before the wind, breaking up the fountains of the great deep, sweeping the whole range of the emotions, as the master hand moves across the harp strings, from the tears and cries of the penitent to the holy laughter and triumphant joy of the cleansed." — Norman Grubb

"We stink more of the world than we stink of sack cloth and ashes. A lot of contemporary churches today would feel more at home in a movie house rather than in a house of prayer, more afraid of holy living than of sinning, know more about money than magnifying Christ in our bodies. It is so compromised that holiness and living a sin-free life is heresy to the modern church. The modern church is, quite simply, just the world with a Christian T-shirt on!" — Nicky Cruz

"You may live in a crowd but you meet God and face eternity alone." — Rees Howells

"The Word says, 'Love not the world, neither the things that are in the world' (1 John 2:15). Jesus warned, 'Beware of covetousness: for a man's life does not consist in the abundance of the things which he possesses' (Luke 12:15). Things —our possessions—can tie us down to this world. While heaven and hell prepare for war, we go shopping. Eternal values are at stake! The end of all we know is near—and we are busy playing with our toys!" — David Wilkerson

"You can tell how popular a church is by who comes on Sunday morning. You can tell how popular the pastor or evangelist is by who comes on Sunday night. But you can tell how popular Jesus is by who comes to the prayer meeting." — Jim Cymbala

ABOUT THE AUTHOR

David Lee Martin is an author, husband, father, and pastor, with a passion to see God move in power in our generation.

You can connect with him through his website, and weekly newsletter, at DavidLeeMartin.com

PRAYER JOURNALS FOR MEN OF GOD

**Spirit-Filled Prayer Journals For Men of Fiery Faith &
Fervent Prayer** with over 200 inspirational Scripture verses
and quotes from great men through the centuries to fuel
your own fervent and faithful prayer life. Enjoy boldly
illustrated motivation straight from the Bible, prayer
prompts and some bonus weapons for your arsenal of
effective prayer!

Buy Your Copy Today

Fearless Prayer Journal for Men

Prayer Journal for Men of God

Available on Amazon

(search prayer journal for men by David Lee Martin)

OTHER BOOKS BY DAVID LEE MARTIN

Discovering The Secret Depths of The Lord's Prayer

Discovering & Developing A Secret Life of Prayer

Discovering & Developing A Passion For God

Printed in Poland
by Amazon Fulfillment
Poland Sp. z o.o., Wrocław

16034178R00103